Mark Ireland was ordain for 14 years as a curate and vicar in Lancashire, before Lichfield Diocesan Missioner. In 2007, he returned to parish ministry and is Vicar of All Saints Wellington with Eyton, in Shropshire. He has co-authored several other books, including *How to Do Mission Action Planning* (SPCK, 2009), the second edition of which is due out in 2016. Mark is a member of the Archbishops' Council. He enjoys walking and skiing with his wife Gill, and is attempting to learn to sail.

Mike Booker has worked in parishes in suburban, urban and rural settings in southern England and the Midlands, as well as for a number of years on the staff of Ridley Hall in the Cambridge Theological Federation. He is currently team rector of a large group of villages on the edge of Cambridge. He is a member of the Church of England's General Synod. With Mark Ireland, Mike was co-author of *Evangelism: Which Way Now?* (Church House Publishing, 2003, 2nd edn 2005). He is married to Liz, with three adult children and a black Labrador.

MAKING NEW DISCIPLES

Exploring the paradoxes of evangelism

Mark Ireland and Mike Booker

First published in Great Britain in 2015

Society for Promoting Christian Knowledge
36 Causton Street
London SW1P 4ST
www.spck.org.uk

British Library Cataloguing-in-Publication Data
A catalogue record for this book is available from the British Library

ISBN 978–0–281–07336–8
eBook ISBN 978–0–281–07337–5

Typeset by Graphicraft Limited, Hong Kong
First printed in Great Britain by Ashford Colour Press
Subsequently digitally printed in Great Britain

eBook by Graphicraft Limited, Hong Kong

Contents

Figures and tables

Figures

Tables

Foreword

The vocation of the Church of Jesus Christ – to proclaim the transforming love of Jesus Christ to the whole world – is unchanging.

However, as with every call of God, it is worked out in real time, in a real place among real lives. This means that our calling is not simply to understand the gospel and to be daily transformed by it, but to engage with the *who, how, where* and *why* so that the proclamation may be as fruitful as possible.

This book is a great help in this task. It is a mapping of the landscape of evangelism over recent decades in this country.

In my experience, many in the Church would prefer to have manuals than maps. Manuals diagnose, dictate and problem-solve. They distil the action necessary by pinpointing the tried-and-tested solution that will invariably bring the change that is desired. But manuals generally deal with machines not people. They are usually most effective in the hands of experts. They are specific to precise models. Of course, we find ourselves desiring such manuals for good reasons, especially when it comes to evangelism. The weight of the calling on us to proclaim the good news effectively is heavy. But the quest to find such a manual (or write such a manual) is in itself a failure to grasp our true calling. It also fundamentally fails to grasp, or be grasped by, the living God.

While I would urge us to stop looking for the manual that will guarantee effective evangelism, I do urge that we seek maps and guides. We need those who will plot the landscape for us, who will point out the well-trodden paths, the routes others have taken and the lessons that have been learned. We need those who can give us peripheral vision to comprehend where we are, how we have got here and what the options are as we move ahead.

This book is such a map. It is a comprehensive guide to the current terrain in evangelism, setting out trends and tools, patterns and practices.

It is my personal conviction that giving attention, energy, resources, thinking, planning and, above all, prayer to the work of evangelism is one of our most urgent tasks. This is not because numbers are falling. It is not because we are doomed if we don't grow. It is not because we are not going to be able to survive unless new people come in to pay for the church roof. It is because of the love of Jesus the Christ. It is the love of Christ that compels us – not fear for our future.

It is this Jesus who teaches us wisdom and urges us to risk. It is this Jesus who urges us to read the signs of the times and not be slow to comprehend. It is this Jesus who followed God's call, and whose Spirit empowers us to do the same.

But the other reason why I value this book and heartily commend it is that it doesn't claim to be a panacea. Whereas a manual offers a generic solution to a generic problem, as if we live in a laboratory with controlled conditions that serve across all circumstances, the Holy Spirit works in particularities. Our following of Jesus Christ, and our invitation to urge family, friends and neighbours to respond to God's call on them to follow, does not happen in ideal conditions. The Holy Spirit engages real people in real time in real circumstances. It is the Holy Spirit who empowers our attempts at witness as well as our accidents, upon whom we are completely reliant. The conditions are only controlled in the sense that God is ultimately the One in control!

The work of proclaiming the good news is indeed our vocation in the Church, but we are entirely reliant on the power of God – to open eyes, turn hearts, bend knees, transform minds and change lives. This book directs us to God as the main player in evangelism: God, who in his infinite grace invites us to partner with him. There is nothing that is more life-giving for a local church than to see people come to faith: for we see the power of the gospel transforming lives, through his power made perfect in our weakness. To be part of the work that God is doing to draw people to Jesus Christ is an awesome privilege and responsibility for which we need wise, experienced and faithful guides. I believe many will find this book to be such a guide.

+ Justin Cantuar:
Lambeth Palace, London

Acknowledgements

———·•◆•·———

This book is the fruit of many conversations, email exchanges and visits. We would like to express our thanks to all those who have shared their wisdom, experiences and insights. We have regularly been humbled and inspired by what God is doing across the country, and by the imagination and commitment of so many people.

In some cases we have made names and locations clear. In others we have not included every detail, but those with whom we have spoken will recognize their stories. However, every person with whom we have been in contact has helped to shape this book, and our thanks are due to each one. In as much as there are mistakes and misunderstandings, they are entirely our own.

In particular we would like to record our appreciation of our colleagues and congregations, who have been tolerant when at times we may have seemed distracted, and especially of our wives, Gill and Liz, for their encouragement and their patience. To these people especially we dedicate this book.

This book is the fruit of shared work. We have pondered and discussed each chapter at length, and both share responsibility for all that is written. To reflect this, we use the first person plural wherever possible. Mark took the lead in undertaking the initial research and writing for Chapters 2, 4, 5, 6, 7, 11 and 13, and Mike for Chapters 1, 3, 8, 9, 10 and 12. At times, we use the first person singular in recording specific conversations, visits or observations that led to the writing of that chapter.

Mark Ireland and Mike Booker

1

The challenge of making new disciples

Today missionary activity still represents the
greatest challenge for the Church.
(Pope John Paul II)

Twelve years ago we wrote a book, *Evangelism: Which Way Now?*[1]
(*EWWN*), with the aim of overviewing what was going on in evangelism
across the churches in England, which strategies and materials were
proving effective, and also what was attracting energy and attention
but maybe having less impact. This was at a time when a major shift
had been going on in understanding how people came to faith. It was
a shift from seeing conversion as a crisis to viewing it as a process
or as a journey. There was also a growing recognition that new
believers needed to be part of healthy and effective churches, and
along with that, an increasingly widespread realization on the part
of far more churches that mission was at the heart of their calling.

The most marked and visible new development in the life of
churches across Britain in the last years of the previous century was
not the national Decade of Evangelism, but one specific venture
launched by one church, the rapidly growing Alpha course. In parallel
with it, a range of other nurture or 'process evangelism' courses
sprang up. The impact upon church life and growth has been
remarkable. Exact quantification is not possible, because those
churches that were taking crowds to hear Billy Graham in the 1950s
to the 1980s are very likely to be the ones most ready to adopt
Alpha or a similar course in the 1990s and beyond. In other words,
where evangelism was going on, more and more of it was being
carried out, with a course of several weeks' duration at its heart.

Alpha was always only a partial answer responding to the need
for a journey to faith that may take several years, with a course

of 15 sessions. In fairness to those who have originated some of the most used courses, they were never intended to be the be all and end all of evangelism. Emmaus Nurture was only part of a series of resources. Alpha comes from a church that makes available a huge range of resources for marriage, parenting, and other elements of Christian living. One of our intentions in writing *EWWN* was to set well-known courses in a wider context of church life and mission. But the reality remains that the main focus of awareness across many churches was on a course of a few weeks, when the journey to faith was always likely to be far longer. If anything, the journey is longer now than it was then, and needs to be undertaken in a more challenging environment.

Changing society, trends and challenges

Rather than simply rewriting and updating, our intention in this book is to look afresh at the scene before us. As authors, we have moved from our previous roles in a diocesan mission post and in theological education to the busyness of parish ministry. With less time for structured research, but more current experience as we write, the book will at times have more personal observation and less research data than our previous publication. As such, we hope that we will be inviting continued discussion and comment.

Surveying the scene as we move further into the twenty-first century, it is clear that subtle but significant changes are under way. The first is the slow but observable progress of secularization. This is expressed in several ways. On one level, it is simply a numerical reality. The Key Points document on religion in England and Wales from the 2011 Census recalls a fall in those who identify as Christian to 59.3 per cent, from 71.7 per cent only ten years earlier. Those reporting no religion have increased from 14.8 per cent to 25.1 per cent over the same time period.[2]

The British Social Attitudes survey 2013 paints a similar picture. The brief section on religious affiliation in the comments:

2

there is little doubt that a substantial change has taken place, with a marked decline in the proportion who describe themselves as belonging to a particular religion. In 1983, around two in three people (68 per cent) considered themselves to belong to one religion or another; in 2012, only around half (52 per cent) do so . . . this decline is in practice a decline in attachment to Anglicanism; in 1983 two in five people (40 per cent) said they were Anglican, and the Church of England could still reasonably lay claim to being England's national church (and thus, arguably, to some extent its fount of moral authority). But now only 20 per cent do so.[3]

At the same time as stated religious allegiance is falling, attendance at Christian worship continues to decline on the part of those who claim to be believers. Not only, it would appear, do fewer people self-identify as believers, but those who do so are less likely to express this in regular worship (see Table 1.1).

Along with falling numbers at church services is the side effect of Christian faith being marginalized from public life. Sometimes this is simple oversight, as Christianity becomes less a 'normal' part of the experience of most people; at other times it takes a more deliberate form. In an interview on national radio recently, a well-known sporting personality was telling the story of his life, and in particular his recovery from alcoholism. Asked to explain what had been instrumental in his recovery, the man replied that

Table 1.1 Attendance at worship by those who claim religious allegiance (percentage)[4]

	1993	2003	2013
Once a week or more	18.9	13.9	13.1
At least once in two weeks	3.2	2.4	2.5
At least once a month	9.0	5.8	6.4
At least twice a year	16.6	10.1	8.4
At least once a year	8.5	5.8	4.2
Less often	6.1	4.3	5.5
Never	36.7	56.7	58.4
Varies	1.0	1.1	1.4

going back to church with his wife had been important. 'Well,' replied the interviewer, 'we can't really talk about that, but what else was important to you?'

The marginalization of Christian discourse from public life can take a more aggressive form. Since 2000, the rise of militant religious belief and associated terrorist acts has led to a growing expression of the view that all religion is not irrelevant but actually harmful. Author Richard Dawkins, until 2008 Professor of the Public Understanding of Science at the University of Oxford, provided intellectual support for a distinctively negative attitude to all religious belief with the publication of *The God Delusion* in 2006.[5] At a rather more down-to-earth level, reality TV personality and *Sun* columnist Katie Hopkins tweeted recently: 'I see that all religion is evil.'[6]

Those working with young people report that similar reactions are increasingly frequent, with religion in general and Christianity in particular seen as repressive, sexist, homophobic and too often associated with child abuse. There is a deep distrust of religion, and for many people that means a distrust of Christianity and, by implication, of Christians. Addressing the Church of England's General Synod in July 2013, the Archbishop of Canterbury observed:

> The social context is changing radically. There is a revolution. It may be, it was, that 59% of the population called themselves Christian at the last census, with 25% saying they had no faith. But the YouGov poll a couple of weeks back was the reverse, almost exactly, for those under 25. If we are not shaken by that, we are not listening.[7]

In place of the religious values that have held sway in the past, the twin trends of consumerism and individualism are summed up by the now familiar saying, 'Tesco ergo sum' (interpreted as 'I shop, therefore I am'). The individual, focused on what can be consumed, is in danger of being not only defined but diminished by the process. As Pope Francis writes: 'The great danger in today's world, pervaded as it is by consumerism, is the desolation and anguish born of a complacent yet covetous heart, the feverish pursuit of frivolous pleasures, and a blunted conscience.'[8]

It is both reassuring and sobering to note that the disconnection between Church and society, and the challenge of taking people on the long journey to full Christian discipleship, is not only an Anglican, English, British or even a Western issue. Bishop Steven Croft, Anglican delegate at the Synod of Bishops in Rome in October 2012, makes the following observation:

> I returned from the Synod of Bishops convinced that the Church all over the world is having the same conversation about the challenge and difficulty of evangelization. I expected to hear about challenge and difficulty from Europe and North America and about growth and hope from Asia, Africa and South America. There were some contrasts but in fact the picture was much more one of challenge in the face of a uniform, powerful, global secularizing culture.[9]

The trends identified in the relationship between the Church and general culture in England are mirrored across the Western world, and are increasingly evident more widely in the Global South. The challenge of this reality to the Church of God across the globe is immense. It may also be that, faced with social trends that have moved further and faster in our own context than in other world regions, lessons learned about effective mission in our increasingly secular context may be of value in other places where the future may hold similar challenges.

The paradox: a longer journey, but less time to commit to it

In the context of a society where Christian faith is less known to many, is perceived as less plausible, and viewed with hostility by a growing minority, a journey of only a few weeks from unbelief to confident faith becomes less and less a realistic expectation. The simple answer, building on recent trends, would be to suggest that the need is for longer courses. However, there seems to be little or no evidence that this is a realistic response.

The challenge is yet greater when looking at other changes going on. Along with being more secular, our culture is becoming busier, with reduced job security encouraging people to accept more demanding work schedules, and leisure time becoming more complex. Concerns about child safety mean that children are increasingly being taken by parents and carers to organized activities. Sunday trading has made its presence felt in a big way, and along with shopping, sports and travel to see family members all take up Sunday time. The switch to smartphone ownership has created a growing proportion of the population who are used to last-minute planning, and far less likely to sign up in advance for long commitments. *Mobile Marketing* online magazine on 24 June 2014 reported a 72 per cent ownership for smartphones across the country. Ownership is now the norm for younger people, but also surprisingly high for those in older age brackets:

> Generation Y – those aged around 25 to 30 – are the most likely to own a smartphone, at 89 per cent, and are considered a key target for mobile marketers. But Generation Z – those aged 16 to 24 – follow closely with 85 per cent smartphone ownership, and these people are the happiest group to use apps for shopping rather than going in store, at 48 per cent. More than half, 54 per cent, of 54 to 65 year olds now own a smartphone too.[10]

Thus, at the same time as the need to take people on a longer journey to faith has become increasingly evident, the readiness of most to commit in advance to a course of any length is decreasing. Life is busier, and long-term planning less of a natural instinct to people who are increasingly ready to respond at short notice to new possibilities. The youth-targeted Alpha publicity video currently in circulation aims to challenge this head on: 'You have approximately 570,000 hours left to live, why not spend less than 24 of them with us on Alpha, exploring life's biggest questions?'[11]

And yet Alpha, beginning with the question, 'Who is Jesus?', no longer finds itself the natural starting point for people who may be searching for faith. Most simply are not at that starting line, ready to move forward. There is undergrowth to be cleared, attention to be raised, before the course can seem like the right next step. Practitioners we have spoken to in preparation for writing this book have reported increasing difficulty in attracting people to join courses. Dedicated and enthusiastic clergy are still using nurture courses very effectively in evangelism, but too often it seems that a high level of personal gifting is needed to attract people to join. It is no longer an easy or a natural process to encourage enquirers to sign up for courses.

New starting points

After the early years of economic confidence, the twenty-first century has seen the biggest economic crisis since the 1930s. Austerity, as a government response to the budget deficit, has hit many hard. Recognizing this, much good work in mission is being done in responding to social needs and working for the common good. In particular, the exponential growth in foodbanks and the work of Christian organizations in debt counselling have done much to live out the authenticity of Christian message. There is, flowing against the stream of suspicion about organized religion and the Church, a clear current of authentic mission in service to those around. In living out the third and fourth of the Anglican Communion's Marks of Mission[12] (to respond to human need by loving service; to seek to transform unjust structures of society, to challenge violence of every kind and to pursue peace and reconciliation), Christians are also preparing the ground for the first and second marks: to proclaim the good news of the kingdom, and to teach, baptize and nurture new believers. Just how well the linkages and mutual resourcing between the different elements of God's mission are working we will explore further in Chapter 11.

Also placed in the early stages of the faith journey are a range of new resources and approaches aimed at allowing open exploration, or at creating fresh spaces for belonging, before the full content of believing has been explored. In particular, resources such as Table Talk (explored in Chapter 7) aim to be accessible to people who are not ready to commit to a longer and more content-laden course. Addressing not only content but the whole context, a wide range of fresh expressions of church, including Messy Church, are playing a significant role in this area. The Church of

England, along with the Methodist Church and other denominations and networks, has recognized the need to train and equip
ministers and ministries with the specific task of pioneering
new work in places, networks and communities untouched by
existing Christian mission. The fundamental question of the nature
of Christian ministry and how best to resource it is rightly under
close scrutiny. Things are changing, and in some areas changing fast,
as the Church recognizes increasingly the scale of the missionary
challenge.

Discipleship, Church and the future

It is not only the start of the journey to full, committed church
membership that is growing in complexity. The loss of knowledge
of the Christian story and the slipping out of our shared life of
Christian practices mean that those who begin the journey
of faith have further to go before they become fully integrated
church members. Or, perhaps to put things in a more positive and
hopeful way, those who begin the journey of discipleship following Jesus Christ will find it harder and take longer to end up as
enthusiastic members of *traditional* churches. The shift from the
early years of the internet to the current multiplicity of social
media has been accompanied by a need to interact and to question, not simply to receive information and to accept it. Evangelism
that sees the faith journey as simply one of inculturation into
existing church life is struggling to make an impact, and is likely
to continue to do so.

Headline figures of church attendance, showing gentle but persistent decline, are only the surface of the story. Beneath that
surface, fresh expressions of church have grown with remarkable
and increasing speed. Spurred on by the *Mission-Shaped Church*
report,[13] a remarkable range of new groups and projects, intended
not to feed people into existing churches but to be new, culturally
relevant churches in their own right, have grown and flourished.
From being the preserve of innovators and enthusiasts, fresh
expressions are now a significant part of the life and membership
of the Church of England, and of the Methodist Church, as the

8

two denominations have worked in partnership to encourage and enable the growth of fresh expressions.

Detailed research carried out by the Church Army[14] is being extended to cover the dioceses of the Church of England. A distinct pattern is emerging of approximately 10 per cent of worshipping Anglicans now being in fresh expressions of church. From very small beginnings at the start of the century, a very significant strand of the life of the Church of God has emerged.

In *EWWN* our overview of approaches to church life and growth left us, as our study progressed, increasingly uneasy at the lack of any programme or resource that was having a significant impact on work with children and young people. It has been heartening to see how in the years that have followed, fresh expressions of church have a far younger age profile than 'inherited' churches. Many aim specifically at families or at young people. Perhaps most significant has been the near-explosive expansion of Messy Church, which works very largely with families and children.

The growth of fresh expressions of church, with the definite intention of growing new churches in their own right and not simply of developing mission projects that will feed people into existing churches, is creating a new dynamic in the life of the whole Church. Since the stated aim is no longer incorporation within current congregations, it raises the question of what these new churches will look like as they mature. In the case of Messy Church, the interactive, participative, exploratory nature of the monthly gathering, including a full shared meal, begs merely one of the most frequently asked questions, which is how involvement in this kind of church can lead to something approaching full participation in 'normal' Sunday worship. Very many fresh expressions are seeing people grow in their church involvement in a way that will not easily sit alongside standard church, or church in 'inherited mode' as it is commonly referred to in literature associated with fresh expressions.

A significant trend that appears to have received insufficient comment to date is the worrying news hidden deep below the surface of those headline church attendance figures. If fresh expressions of church have grown and are continuing to grow, their inclusion in the total record of church membership masks a profoundly disturbing trend: attendance at 'inherited mode' churches is falling far faster than national totals might indicate. As new and exciting ventures make up some of the losses, the number of worshippers in 'church as we have known it' is declining at a rate that remains deeply worrying. Even in a climate far more ready to acknowledge the scale of the challenge facing the Church than has been the case to date, the speed at which traditional churches are losing members does not appear to be fully grasped.

Since the Church of England, along with the other historic denominations and national churches of the Western world, still has the great bulk of its financial and human resources (if measured by paid clergy) invested in inherited mode churches, enthusiasm for fresh expressions should not eclipse completely the need for a very hard look at what can be done to enable standard churches to flourish. There will always be some that flourish, usually because they are led by exceptionally gifted clergy and lay leaders. It has been our privilege to talk to some of these in researching this book. But exceptional leaders are by definition a minority and cannot necessarily point the way for good, prayerful, dedicated but averagely human leaders to follow.

One way the 16,000 churches of the Church of England have a huge range of opportunities for contact with their surrounding populations is through what the church calls 'occasional offices'. These are services that may indeed happen occasionally, or actually very regularly in busy parishes. The name references the fact that they take place because of special occasions – baptisms, weddings and funerals. Although also declining in number, they remain highly significant.

In 2013 the Church of England baptized over 130,000 people (2,500 per week), of which 80,000 were infants and 42,000 were children aged between one and 12. There were 50,000 marriages in Church of England churches, and 160,000 funerals conducted by Anglican ministers.[15] Added together, the time spent in responding with sensitivity and care to each of these occasions represents a very significant part of the established Church's energies. Research for the Diocese of London purports to show a clear inverse correlation nationally between the number of occasional offices and the propensity for churches to grow numerically.[16] London Diocese, with the lowest number of funerals per member of clergy, shows the strongest national growth.

Since it is not an option for a national Church to refuse to take funerals, baptisms or weddings – and it would be highly insensitive for any other denomination too – the task facing the Church is to respond as well as possible, and to see pastoral care and mission completely intertwined. Used well, occasional offices can be a major source of mission opportunity for inherited mode church. They allow contact with those who might not otherwise approach a church, and can reach far into the national population in a way that parallels, but is often quite distinct from, the impact of fresh expressions of church. We will look further at the effective missional use of occasional offices in Chapter 10.

Along with a number of other fresh expressions of church, Messy Church normally envisages a main meeting only once a month. This is a departure from the historic Christian norm of meeting weekly for worship on the first day of the week. The first reference to Sunday worship in the New Testament is in Acts 20.7, recalling Paul's meeting with the Ephesian elders in Troas. There may have been a pragmatic reason for this particular meeting, but the pattern of weekly worship draws also on the Jewish tradition of Sabbath observance, affirmed repeatedly through the Old Testament. The weekly pattern of worship would appear to date to the earliest years of the Church, and it is a significant step to move away from this.

The significance of weekly worship is not just historical. Robin Gill, in *Churchgoing and Christian Ethics*,[17] provides strong statistical evidence that those who worship weekly in church have significantly higher levels of belief in God, in the divinity of Christ and in the authority of the Bible. They are also more likely to be altruistic, and less likely to hold racist views. Monthly attenders, on the other hand, have patterns of belief and behaviour little different from the general population. This indicates a need to be hesitant about the value of new expressions of church activity that are based upon monthly involvement. But questioning only fresh expressions of church on these grounds is unfair. A parallel development in church attendance patterns has been a marked and increased shift to less frequent, perhaps monthly, worship on the part of those who may view themselves as fully committed members of inherited mode churches. The infrequent attendance phenomenon seems to be one facing the whole Church.

Falling regularity in church attendance, combined with fresh expressions of church that may meet just once a month, will spell disaster for the Church if attendance at shared worship is indeed the main way people grow as disciples of Jesus Christ. Fortunately, the picture is not as simple as that. Attempting to identify the drivers behind the link he identifies between church attendance, attitudes and behaviour, Robin Gill comments: 'Churchgoing fosters and sustains a distinctive culture, and therefore, can sustain a sense of personal identity.'[18] It may be that other routes into discipleship will increasingly take up this role, replacing weekly church worship.

The Revd Kate Bottley has written in *The Guardian* about the pressures on time people face, and the reasons for declining regularity in attending church:[19]

> Those who can come do, but I always get some texts back. Last week it was, 'Sorry, away this weekend on the bikes,' and 'Won't be there, visiting Santa.' A family bringing their child for baptism recently asked if they could have him 'done' on a Saturday because his little sister always has gymnastics competitions on Sundays.

There may be validity in the reasoning here, but discussion below the online edition revealed the scepticism of many observers. One of the most popular comments stated:

> In terms of the idea that people are now too time pressured to go to church, do you really think people in the days before the limited hours working week, the two day weekend, etc., were less time pressured? I'm not virulently anti-religion, and a lot of clergy do some great community and pastoral work. I just think the root cause of less people going to church is less people seeing it as a relevant part of their lives.

Christians believe, at least in theory, that following Jesus is not only relevant but absolutely vital. What would appear to be important is that the Church, whatever its form of meeting or of worship, and however frequently people attend formal worship, is a place in which people are enabled to see the world differently, to be inspired to live otherwise. It is to be a place (in the very broadest sense) in which a journey as disciples of Jesus Christ is undertaken. If it is not achieving that, then staying at home having a Sunday lie-in is indeed probably time well spent. That process of becoming and following as a disciple certainly can be forwarded by regular Sunday worship, as has been the case historically. However, this seems to be declining as the mainstay of discipleship, so the need grows to consider how growing as committed disciples of Jesus can be related to every part of life.

Discipleship: the live question

The Bible translator J. B. Phillips once famously described his experience of working on a fresh translation of the New Testament as being 'continually struck by the living quality of the material' on which he is working. Some will, no doubt, consider it merely superstitious reverence for 'Holy Writ', yet again and again the writer felt rather like 'an electrician rewiring an ancient house without being able to turn the mains off'.[20]

Working not only with inspired Scripture but with the passions and experiences of a wide range of Christians seeking God's way forward in the life of the Church, we have in some small way had a similar experience. Time and time again the subject of discipleship has emerged in conversation, as a theme being pondered by practitioners across a wide range of Christian groups and activities. At the same time as new questions are being identified as to how contacts can become genuine and lifelong disciples, the ineffectiveness of much current church life in enabling discipleship is also recognized.

The fact that discipleship has until now been both reflected and shaped by regular Sunday worship does not necessarily mean that the future will see most believers following Jesus more closely by doing the same things in the same ways. Taking stock of the current landscape, we have identified a number of paradoxes. The journey is longer, as we have seen, but time to commit to it is less easy to find. Busy church members need well-produced resources and easily usable packages, but a thirst for authenticity will lead people to be suspicious of anything that looks too slick or mass produced.

The journey to wholehearted faith and commitment can most certainly be encouraged by an understanding of the journey as far longer – as evidenced, for example, in the explicit targeting of much of the Pilgrim course to disciples rather than to enquirers. We will look more closely at this in Chapter 7. However, there are wider questions to be addressed, including the very nature of the Church, of ministry and of what mature and growing discipleship really looks like.

In the Bible, the call of Jesus to 'follow me' is repeatedly made. Those who join him are called so that they might be *with* him, but also so that they may be *sent out* to preach and to defeat evil (Mark 3.13–15). Clearly, this implies being with one another, and the growth of the Early Church provides New Testament evidence of the fundamental significance of the Christian community. Nevertheless, the call of Jesus is primarily one to share the journey with him, and to be sent in service and proclamation from the very beginning. Disciples are those who learn from Jesus' teaching, in relationship with him and with one another, but also those who learn from the start by doing.

As we explore in the next chapter, discipleship through learning alone has a limited effect. Catechesis – the teaching of the faith – is vital, but the learning of the faith comes also through living faith, testing faith and sharing faith. The different elements of church life and mission explored in this book are only part of what is going on, but focus on key areas and approaches where life, energy and hope are to be found. Within nearly all, there is evidence of discipleship being expressed in a remarkable range of ways. Experienced believers are growing as disciples as they put their faith to work in new ways, while others are being drawn to share in the discipleship journey, even though they may still have very many questions and be far from a traditional world-view.

Some of the priorities identified in this book have already been seen and addressed in realistic ways by a number of Church of England dioceses and in other denominations. Strategic planning at high levels will be of great importance as major financial and personnel pressures have to be faced. Far more significantly, dioceses, churches and denominations proclaiming mission as a gospel priority, and not just as a means to survival, is a cause of very great encouragement and a significant move from the position a generation ago. Our purpose in writing is different: we aim to provide an overview of things that are happening and may be accessed at the level of the local church. As well as looking at facts and figures, we are trying to tell stories, to share experiences of what it can be like in ordinary local settings. Our hope is that, in providing a wide overview of what is happening, we will help Christians and churches to make connections, to see how evidence of life and growth in one way can link in with more life and new growth in another. We want to share news of how people are becoming disciples, growing as disciples, and living out that discipleship, even in the face of the changes and challenges of a fast-moving culture.

2

The priority: growing the Church or growing people?

If we don't disciple, then the culture sure will, and it's doing a good job of it. Consumerism is the alternative religion of our day . . . Everyone who comes to Christ in a Western culture is already a well discipled consumer.

(Alan Hirsch)

It is [Christ] whom we proclaim, warning everyone and teaching everyone in all wisdom, so that we may present everyone mature in Christ. For this I toil and struggle.

(Colossians 1.28–29)

Last summer I started to learn to sail. This was something almost completely new to me, but having talked to friends who were keen sailors I had always fancied having a go, and when I saw a taster day at a local sailing club advertised for the date of my birthday, I finally decided to give it a try.

I met some really great people down at the club. But the first time I turned up at the club wasn't a great success – I capsized! – and the second time I ended up in the wrong group by mistake. I could easily have dropped out altogether at that point, but then a chap called Mike took me under his wing and began to show me the ropes. After that first meeting he turned up week in, week out, whatever the weather, in case I was there, to take me out for a sail. And he never said to me, 'I'd rather be doing some proper sailing . . .'

Eventually he said, 'Now it's time for me to get out of the boat; next time I'll stay on the land and watch.' What Mike has been doing is mentoring me. I could have said that Mike has been discipling me, though he wouldn't recognize the word. But Mike has taught me a lot about discipling, because his example has shown me how people learn to follow Jesus – when someone gets alongside them, makes friends, encourages and guides them.

In the face of the difficult and challenging context outlined in the previous chapter, the temptation to focus on displacement activities rather than on making new disciples is immense. As Archbishop Justin Welby acknowledged in his first presidential address to General Synod:

> We need new imagination in evangelism through prayer, and a fierce determination not to let evangelism be squeezed off our agendas. At times I feel it's rather like me when I have to write a difficult letter, or make an awkward phone call: even things like ironing my socks become more attractive. We treat evangelism too often in the same way. We will talk about anything . . . and we struggle to fit in the call to be the good news in our times through Jesus Christ.

And yet if members of a sailing club can be so passionate in sharing the joy of sailing, and so dedicated in teaching people how to sail, which is just one satisfying recreation among many, how much more should we as Christians be passionate and dedicated about passing on what we have learned about Jesus, who is the Saviour of the world? And if we long to see our consumerist and individualist society transformed by the values of God's kingdom, how can we not be passionate about making new disciples who will share with us in working for justice and promoting the common good?

At the end of my first season in the sailing club the commodore came up to chat to me, and asked, 'Will you sign up for next year?' I thanked him for his encouragement and said how struck I was by the huge amount of effort and time the experienced members of the club put in to teach beginners like me to sail, when they could be out enjoying themselves competing with each other. He explained that they were all happy to pass on their skills, and the only way to maintain a large and flourishing club was to work constantly at recruiting new members, as every year quite a number of members dropped out for various reasons – some moved away, others had children growing up and developing other hobbies, others left because of health or work. I asked how many of the 20 new recruits they had trained that summer would rejoin the following year. He replied, 'Probably two or three; we reckon about 10 per cent. What might make you decide to keep it up?' I immediately thought about my parish's work in baptism preparation, where we are discouraged by a similarly small level of continuing involvement, but have generally put in rather less one-to-one time in building up relationships with newcomers than happens at the sailing club. I don't know if the commodore has a faith, but he has definitely challenged me about my commitment to evangelism!

Growing the church or growing people?

Of course, declining levels of membership and commitment are a feature of society, not just the church – the British Social Attitudes survey shows the decline in membership of the three main political parties is at least as steep as that of the churches. It is tempting for a church that recognizes it is in long-term decline to make growing the numbers the top priority. However, doing this is to make the motivation for evangelism institution-centred rather than people-centred – seeking to make new disciples for the sake of the church rather than for the sake of the lost. This is what missiologists such as Johannes Verkuyl would describe as an 'impure' motive for mission.[1]

Rather, in this chapter we want to explore the paradox that the best way to grow the Church is to focus not on numerical growth but on growing disciples. As Robert Warren affirms, 'The best way to grow the church is to grow people.' This is an aim that draws together what the Church has so often separated, namely evangelism and discipleship. Yet when people are growing in confidence, in skills for life and becoming more like Jesus, then their faith will naturally spill out in their relationships and draw others in. And a church that is focused on growing people is likely to be more attractive to the unchurched and the seeker than one that is focused on growing in order to perpetuate itself.

Warren comments that if, in the life of the Church, we took the primary goal as growing people, this would do a number of things:

- It would set before every member the goal, and call, to be growing as people throughout our lives and in all aspects of them.
- It is a multifaceted goal as it includes growing in our relationship with God, with ourselves in personal honesty, integrity and awareness, and also in growing in our relationships with others.
- Those 'relationships with others' cover a wide spectrum of aspects of growth, such as personal/family relationships, church membership, work and leisure relationships, and the wider dimensions of social, cultural and political relationships. In so doing, people can be helped to see the truth that living as a follower of Christ is not primarily about 'going to church' but 'going with God into the whole of life'. It is essentially a life-affirming move. The real 'leaders' of the church become those who are living life before God to the full, rather than necessarily 'full-time church workers'.
- In so far as we can be effective in moving in the direction of 'growing people', for example to be good listeners, to be people who stand up for those who are overlooked in any grouping, or who are living out of a sense of *vocation*, rather than *driven-ness*, we are likely to provoke others to ask us for 'a reason for the hope that is in us'.
- It is this that is likely to be the best basis for evangelism because people will be seeing something of the good news worked out by our approach to life.
- Also, it essentially looks out towards life and the world around us, rather than inwards to the church and its structures and ways of operating.[2]

Growing people grow disciples

Growing people grow other people. Unless the most mature and committed disciples in the Church feel that they themselves are growing and being fulfilled through membership of their local church they will not be at their best at bringing new people into the Church and nurturing them in their faith. Given that each of the Gospels ends with a call from Jesus to his disciples to disciple others,[3] one might think it taken for granted that being a true disciple of Jesus involves making new disciples. In his helpful book *Real-life Discipleship*, American pastor Jim Putman defines a disciple as one who follows Jesus, is being changed by Jesus and is committed to the mission of Jesus.[4] However, in the literature about discipleship in this country, it is possible to read otherwise excellent books that fail to mention that a key aspect of Jesus-shaped mission is not only deepening our own discipleship but also learning to disciple others.[5]

Discipling people does not mean squeezing people to fit into their local church. The mission of the Church is its calling to share in the mission of God the Father to restore the fallen creation to him through Jesus Christ and in the power of the Holy Spirit, making manifest his kingdom.[6] Mission is about being sent – sent by a God who is a missionary. This mission of God (*missio Dei*) is cosmic in scope, encompassing the struggle for justice, peace and the integrity of creation, and flows out of the nature of the Trinity as a fount of sending love. As *Mission-Shaped Church* puts it, 'It is not the Church of God that has a mission to the world, but the God of Mission who has a Church in the world.'[7]

Although, as we explained in *EWWN*, mission is wider than just evangelism, the mission of God is not being undertaken in all its fullness unless people are called to become disciples of Jesus Christ. In the New Testament the making of new disciples seems to arise not so much from 'ought' as from 'overflow'. The motivation to proclaim the faith and make new disciples arises from our response to the grace of God shown to us in Jesus Christ – what M. Thomas Thangaraj describes as 'loving gratitude'. Or, as Johannes van den Berg put it, drawing on 2 Corinthians 5.14, we are 'constrained by Jesus' love'.[8]

If we make growing people our aim, rather than growing the Church, then we will be much closer to the example of Jesus himself. In the Gospels it is striking, given such a short period of public ministry, how much time Jesus devotes to growing his core leaders and to one-to-one encounters with people on the edge. We shall look at this more closely in the next chapter.

'Doing' discipleship or growing people?

Discipleship as a key area in church life has already received a lot of attention.[9] Many excellent discipleship courses have been produced, as we shall explore in Chapter 7. Yet the paradox is that despite all this energy going into creating and promoting discipleship resources, churches generally still do not seem to be getting noticeably better at making whole-life disciples who will in turn disciple others. George Barna, writing from his research in the USA, observes: 'Almost every church in our country has some type of discipleship program, or set of activities, but stunningly few churches have a church of disciples.'[10] Or, as Alan Hirsch has commented:

> The Church in the West has largely forgotten the art of disciple-making and has largely reduced it to an intellectual assimilation of theological ideas. As a result, we have a rather anaemic cultural Christianity highly susceptible to the lures of consumerism . . . In our desire to be seeker-friendly and attractional, we have largely abandoned the vigorous kind of discipleship that characterised early Christianity and every significant Jesus movement since.[11]

Barna's research identifies a number of reasons why churches have failed to produce distinctive disciples. The first of these is that while the majority of Christians said that having a deep, personal commitment to the Christian faith was a high priority for the future, when asked what they hoped to accomplish in life (without suggesting specifics), only one in five mentioned anything directly related to spiritual outcomes. Barna concludes that committed Christians feel that they have already arrived spiritually – 'they view their challenge as one of spiritual maintenance rather than of spiritual development'.[12]

21

The Church of England's recent research project, *From Anecdote to Evidence*,[13] cites some alarming findings concerning the priority – or lack of it – attached by even committed Christians to passing on their faith to their children. Evidence from the European Values Study shows that among those Anglicans who say that religion is 'very important' in their lives, only 36 per cent listed religious faith as an especially important quality that children can be encouraged to learn at home, compared to good manners (94 per cent) or tolerance and respect (83 per cent).[14] If committed church members don't see the importance of communicating the faith even to their own children, it clearly illustrates how far we are from creating a culture of disciple-making disciples.

Sitting watching my grandson eat his lunch as I write leaves me pondering. What do I most long for in his life as it stretches out before him? Good health, certainly. Academic success, a rewarding career and happy family life would be good too. But is that what truly matters? Above all else, I long for him to know he is a child of God, and to live life in all its fullness following Jesus. If we believe that life as a disciple is life at its best, there is nothing of greater importance we can desire for those we treasure most in the next generation.

'A community of missionary disciples'

This attractive definition of the Church is taken from the 2013 Roman Catholic Apostolic Letter, *Evangelii Gaudium*, where it is a recurring theme.[15] Although for too long the Church has tended to restrict the word 'ministry' to work undertaken by those – ordained or lay – who are trained and authorized by the hierarchy, there is now a growing ecumenical and international rediscovery of the Church as the whole baptized people of God called to mission and sustained by the Eucharist. Or, to put it another way, the Church is the community of disciples called to be together with Jesus and sent out (Mark 3.14).

Disciples are not formed primarily through courses or training events. Jesus did not invite his disciples to come on a course, but to enter into life. As Roger Walton argues, disciples are formed primarily through mission, through worship and through community – through being with Jesus and being sent out.[16] In this context it is good to be reminded that 40 per cent of Anglican fresh expressions of church are currently led by lay people with no formal theological training or authorization.[17] While traditional models of residential training still have their place, an increasing number of ordinands, and not only pioneer leaders in fresh expressions, value training that is relevant and contextual – to be mentored on the job, rather than sent away to study.

Transformation of a person's whole life, including his or her values, lifestyle, world-view and vocation, tends to be most effectively done one to one in an intentional mentoring relationship. Nowadays all sorts of people have a mentor or coach, from CEOs of large organizations to newly qualified teachers, or troubled teenagers in danger of reoffending. Yet one place you may struggle to find a personal mentor or coach is your local church, despite Jesus Christ being the all-time exemplar of the servant-coach.

Many of the caring professions work within a very different culture from that of most Christian ministry. Being married to somebody who has recently qualified as a psychotherapeutic counsellor has brought home the difference. For a counsellor, regular supervision is not an option but simply a mandatory part of the job. Not only general approaches to professional practice, but specifically each individual client, are considered on a regular and frequent basis with a trained supervisor. Meanwhile, members of clergy may share a pint with a wise friend or see a spiritual director every few weeks, but a professional culture of supervision is still a long way off.

Growing believers one to one

The assumption that getting people more involved in church activities and courses will automatically help them grow spiritually is challenged by the 'Reveal' research, undertaken by Willow Creek, a large church in Chicago that has pioneered 'seeker-friendly' services. The research into how its congregation was growing spiritually, conducted between 2004 and 2007, tested the hypothesis that 'the more a person far from God participates in church activities, the more likely it is that those activities will produce a person who loves God and loves others'. The study found this assumption to be invalid. The researchers divided church attenders into four groups, according to their stage of spiritual formation.

- *Exploring Christ* – 'I believe in God, but I am not sure about Christ. My faith is not a significant part of my life.'
- *Growing in Christ* – 'I believe in Jesus and I am working on what it means to get to know him.'
- *Close to Christ* – 'I feel really close to Christ and depend on him daily for guidance.'
- *Christ-centred* – 'My relationship with Jesus is the most important relationship in my life. It guides everything I do.'

The research showed that courses and activities did work, but only for those in the first two (less committed) groups. The more mature Christians (those in the last two categories, comprising more than a quarter of the church's congregation) tended to be stalled in their spiritual growth (particularly the 'close to Christ' group) or dissatisfied with what the church was doing to help them grow (mostly those in the fourth, most committed group). The church and its ministries were helping people in the earlier stages of their Christian lives, but the programme of the church increasingly disappointed people as their faith developed, and many in the last group were considering leaving. Without realizing it, this very large and 'successful' church was providing the least support for those who were most active in sustaining its activities and ministries.[18]

The publication of the findings has sparked a lively debate on both sides of the Atlantic, regarding its research methodology and also the strengths and weakness of so-called 'seeker services'.[19] If this research had been restricted to one American mega-church it would be easy to dismiss it as showing the flaws of a particular model; however, the research team went on to examine 200 other US churches, with very similar findings.

While church life is very different – and so much smaller in scale – in Britain, it is worth asking whether it might be true here too that churches tend to take for granted their most committed and hard-working members. Perhaps this contributes not only to the stalling of the spiritual growth of local churches, but to the gradual build-up of resentment and frustration, which only comes to the surface when a faithful leader suddenly erupts and resigns, all too often leaving the church as well. We have also noticed how parents will get heavily involved in a church with good children's work as long as their children are around, but once the children have moved on the parents can very easily drop out of church life. This may be a sign of the deep concern those parents have for their children to grow in the faith, such that they are willing to be 'used' by the church even if they themselves are not growing spiritually; but once the children have left, they re-evaluate the cost and benefit of belonging to such a church.

Most clergy are familiar with and value the ministry of a spiritual director or soul friend, in whom they can regularly confide, and to whom they can make themselves accountable. Given their own positive experience, it is perhaps worth asking why more of us as ministers do not seek to make this kind of one-to-one mentoring available to our most committed members. It may be more helpful to them than asking already overcommitted lay leaders to sign away another evening a week or precious Saturday for a discipleship course.

Connecting with seekers one to one

One-to-one mentoring is not only key for discipling long-standing and committed church members, it is increasingly important in nurturing those taking their very first steps as enquirers exploring the claims of Christianity. In a recent lecture, Rico Tice, director of evangelism at All Souls, Langham Place and author of the evangelistic course Christianity Explored, described how that leading evangelical church has had to change its strategy. In 1954, around the time Billy Graham came to Harringay Stadium, people were converted through a single sermon. By 1994, when

Rico joined All Souls, people were much further back on the road and there were a number of stumbling blocks that needed to be overcome before they could respond to the gospel – so they developed Christianity Explored. They found that as long as they put on monthly guest services and arranged for a new course to start just after each guest service, then people would bring themselves along and a steady trickle of people became Christians.

These days, however, that strategy is no longer working as effectively as it used to. Tice says:

> People are not just further back along the road, they are on a different road altogether. I am no longer getting them on a course unless first a friend brings them to a guest service, and then afterwards on the way home, the friend talks to them about what they have heard and asks, 'What did you make of that? Would you like to have a look at the source document with me?'[20]

It is the friend who follows up after the guest service who is the decisive factor in whether the person eventually signs up for the course. This observation is significant, coming from someone who is himself a passionate exponent of process evangelism courses, but who recognizes that in our changing culture one-to-one discipling is essential alongside offering courses.

One's own theological tradition may be rather different from that of All Souls, with its guest services and courses, but there is a question here about the place of personal invitation that is relevant across all traditions. How can regular worshippers be given the confidence to invite their friends to come to church? The church's year provides a series of special occasions or festivals when someone who really enjoys coming to church could pass a simple invitation card to their friend at the school gate or work colleague with the words, 'I'm going. It'll be good. Would you like to come with me?'

From distrust to discipleship

Meeting individually with non-Christians is all the more important in a culture where organized religion is increasingly distrusted and even seen as immoral. Until a person has formed a friendship with a Christian whose life shows integrity and is someone that person is willing to trust, attempts to explain the Christian message tend to fall on deaf ears. We live in a society that has painfully learned that institutions are not necessarily to be trusted, and in this climate of distrust the process of making new disciples is likely to take much longer and involve overcoming significant barriers before the Christian message will even be given a hearing of any sort.

In *Pathway to Jesus*,[21] Don Everts and Doug Schaupp analyse the stories of 2,000 postmoderns who have come to faith on college campuses in the USA. They identify that the process of conversion for postmoderns is both mysterious and organic, and includes crossing five thresholds, each of which seems huge until you have crossed it; but for those who have already crossed to faith they seem no big deal:

- *From distrust to trust*: getting to know and actually trusting someone who is a Christian.
- *From complacent to curious*: becoming curious about Jesus.
- *From being closed to change in their life to being open to change in their life*: in the authors' experience, almost always the hardest to cross; the stage that needs the most prayer.
- *From meandering to seeking*: from endlessly exploring alternatives to positively seeking answers in Jesus.
- *Crossing the threshold of the kingdom itself*: while earlier thresholds need a pressure-free process, a challenge to commit needs to be made now.

The fifth threshold looks old-fashioned and familiar – the difference for postmoderns is the significance of the four previous thresholds that need to be crossed first. The authors also stress from their experience the priority of intensive one-to-one mentoring in the eight weeks after the commitment has been made. This first threshold also ties in with other research suggesting that 'approximately 77 per cent of the persons who become Christian disciples do so because of the testimony, deeds, and encouragement of someone they trust'.[22]

If only I had the time . . .

Clergy and ministers have traditionally had a key role in making disciples one to one. In John Finney's research for *Finding Faith Today*, a relationship with the minister was identified as a key factor by people who had come to Christian faith – cited by converts as the second most common 'main factor', and also as the most common 'supporting factor'.[23] Discipling is a skill that is learned by example rather than from the pulpit, yet with falling numbers of stipendiary clergy and churches being joined together into ever larger groups, time to spend individually discipling church members and seekers on an intentional basis is becoming more difficult to find. As parish clergy, we find again and again that when ministers are asked to take on responsibility for more churches, they may well be able to manage the extra administration, but at the cost of having less time to grow individual people.

In the original research commissioned by the Church Commissioners, *From Anecdote to Evidence*, a clear link was identified between an increase in the number of churches looked after by a priest and the decline in church attendance across the benefice as a whole: 'There is a strong negative trend between the more churches amalgamated together and the likelihood of decline (across all categories of church size).' The report goes on to say: 'In 2011 (most recent statistics), 71% of the Church of England's parishes were in multi-parish teams or benefices. In 1960 the figure was only 17%.'[24] This uncomfortable finding has led to further research being undertaken, and the debate about whether correlation is a sign of causality will doubtless continue.

After I arrived in my rural benefice, Comberton saw several years of steady growth. When I then took on responsibility for further parishes the life of the church continued to flourish, but it was far harder to achieve numerical growth. The simple reality is that changing to a model where growth is maintained with less clergy time is by no means an easy process.

Reimagining small groups for discipleship

So may belonging to a small group be the key to genuine discipleship? It depends. When we wrote *EWWN*, many churches were exploring cell church as a way of making small groups central to growing disciples. Our conclusion then was that while this model seems to work well in other cultures, we could find little evidence of it being effective in a British context. Twelve years on, we feel our verdict still stands. It is significant that tools for discipleship that arise from a UK context, such as Alpha and Messy Church, have proved hugely effective, while models from overseas, such as cell church and seeker services, have not.

Yet it seems that even the British style of home groups or fellowship groups largely fails to produce consistent and significant transformation of individuals in most church contexts. Part of the reason for this is that small groups tend to focus on imparting knowledge (including those that concentrate on Bible study) or on pastoral support (providing safe space, a listening ear and prayer support) rather than equipping members to hold each other to account for their spiritual growth and behaviour. Part of the genius of early Methodist 'band' meetings was the encouragement and freedom to ask each other quite demanding personal questions about sin, temptation and spiritual growth – along the lines of 'How goes it with your soul?'

Without such a clear agenda for personal growth, small groups tend to maintain people where they are, rather than move them on towards personal holiness and growth. A classic sign of a group that has plateaued is one that would prefer not to have new members, either because they might upset the relationships of trust within the group or because the room isn't big enough and the group is unwilling to face the cost involved in splitting into two. Once a group is not inclined to accommodate new members it is unlikely to be able to play a part in helping the church to grow.

A new home group coordinator was appointed in a large, successful church in the Midlands, who quickly identified that many of the groups had been spiritually stuck for years. It was decided to dissolve all existing home groups and form new groups. In the run-up to the change the home group coordinator became the most unpopular person in the church, and was bombarded with complaints, but she held her nerve. But, within a few months of the change having taken place all the complaints were forgotten, and most people said it was the best thing that had happened in the life of the church.

A useful resource

- **Mentor Connect** – a new national initiative (from CPAS, the Evangelical Alliance and Stewardship), enabling leaders of churches and Christian organizations to connect with carefully selected leadership mentors (<www.mentorconnect.org.uk>).

3

Strategy or spontaneity?

————◆•◆————

How do you make God laugh? Tell him your future plans.

Events, dear boy, events.
(Harold Macmillan's reported response to a journalist who
asked what is most likely to blow governments off course)

In exploring some of the paradoxes currently facing the local church
in evangelism, much of our focus will be upon resources, strategies
and possible plans. And yet, as experience repeatedly shows, first
contact with reality is likely to throw even the most careful plans
off course. In the next two chapters, we look more closely at the
balance between God's work and human activity in making new
disciples. Some questions of the interplay between the divine and
the human will be left for further pondering. In this chapter our
focus is on how we balance the need for planning with the reality
that life will constantly bring fresh challenges and opportunities
that even the most thorough planning could not foresee.

For many local churches, the idea of goals and plans can still seem
alien, an inappropriate intrusion into church culture. For generations, the local church has simply been 'there', its very existence
seen as sufficient in itself. This was always an inadequate answer,
but its weakness is now exposed more explicitly in the light of the
rapid cultural changes we explored in Chapter 1. Those who aim at
nothing will end up hitting their target. As we know from the natural
world, the survival of any given species depends on its ability to
change at a rate at least as fast as that of its surroundings.

Ironically, aiming at too much can be as ineffective as aiming
at nothing. Churches with a global theological vision, for example
making disciples of all nations, or bringing about the kingdom
of God, place before themselves an ideal that simply cannot be

achieved by one church within one lifetime. Serious commitment to that vision needs to be focused into achievable goals, although what is achievable must also be explored and stretched through faith-filled prayer.

There is a need, therefore, for strategies that focus upon realistic goals. They can and should be shaped by a broader vision, but aim to establish achievable steps towards the realization of that vision. In recent years, the process of Mission Action Planning has been widely adopted by many dioceses in the Church of England (although, interestingly, far less so in other denominations) as a framework within which to set a strategic direction. Having been in use long enough and sufficiently widely for clear statistical trends to be identified, Bob Jackson's recent research leads him to conclude: 'The accumulated evidence strongly suggests that MAP is associated with improving numerical growth trends.'[1]

Looking further at Mission Action Planning

Starting with the Diocese of London's Agenda for Action in 1993, the development of what have generally become known as Mission Action Plans (MAPs) has spread across most dioceses of the Church of England. The nature of a MAP has been outlined in the following definition:

> A 'Mission Action Plan' is a document which outlines the mission activities that a local church is going to do in the coming months and years. It is built on a clear sense of God's 'vision' for the church – what God is calling the church to be and to do. So a MAP provides exactly what it says on the tin – an action plan for mission.[2]

Building on the process of strategic planning that will be familiar to many in professional settings, MAPs bring in a specific focus on mission. If any action is to be in the plan, it needs to be mission-focused. This is significant, because much busyness in church life can carry on unconnected to mission, can be considered important because it has always been done and can soak up energy unquestioned. Exposing this may be painful, but perhaps also a relief, since keeping on with all that has previously been done while also grappling with the challenge to reach out in mission can leave a congregation feeling helpless in the face of the scale of the task. A good MAP will help chart the best way forward, and in doing so will bring about the realization that not everything can or should be done, taking a great weight of anxiety off many shoulders. Having an agreed MAP gives churches a way to say no to good ideas and competing agendas, and can also help them to think more long term – most churches overestimate what can be achieved in a year and underestimate what can be achieved in five years.

Planning for the Plan

Encouragingly, very few diocesan websites give detailed descriptions or examples of specific completed MAPs. The introduction is nearly always to the *process* of planning. The plan itself is certainly important, but the process of arriving at it is at least as significant. That's because it is in discussing who we are, what we are called to do, and how we might do it, that shared understanding grows. In summary, the process will need to involve four stages, revolving around a continued commitment to immerse each stage in prayer (see Figure 3.1, from Mark Ireland and Mike Chew's book):

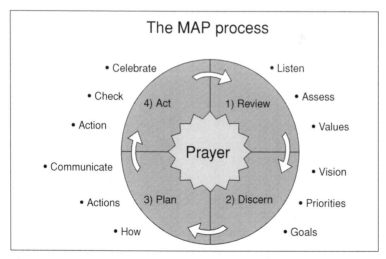

Figure 3.1 An illustration of the MAP process[3]

1 Review your situation.
2 Discern future priorities.
3 Make plans.
4 Act on the plans.

The more open and consultative the planning process, the greater will be the range of insights, and – if the process is managed effectively – the greater will be the ownership of the plan once it begins to be put into action.

The Diocese of Southwark puts it well:

> A Mission Action Plan (MAP) is a process of strategic planning which reflects on opportunities and resources available to a local church and informs a strategy to direct activities and decision making over the coming years. The heart of MAP is the *process* by which a church comes to understand its mission and put that into effect, rather than the *product* of a document.[4]

Shared planning can include spontaneity. It will do so if it is genuinely and deliberately shared, and does not include only those who enjoy planning. The setting can help in this, for example working through informal gatherings over meals as well as more structured meetings. Some of the most valuable people in the planning process will be the ones who least want to be there. They will be already committed to action, longing just to 'get on with it', and often better able to see what God is doing in and around them at that very moment. In bringing their insights, gifts and personalities to play alongside the instinctive strategic thinkers and planners, a plan can emerge that already draws in the life and spontaneity of the intuitive thinkers and activists of the church.

Two vicars go to the supermarket

In the shared process of writing this book, our conversations sometimes strayed to other things. Over a meal, we found ourselves discussing how we approached going shopping. One of us had a menu prepared, a shopping list, and a strategy of seeking advice from supermarket staff until every necessary item had been found. The other tended to roll up at the store, see what was on offer or looked especially tasty, and mentally started planning menus in the light of what was there. Those who know us will have no difficulty in working out who is who! One was in danger of missing out on new ideas and special offers. The other would actually end up being more adventurous if time was spent with a recipe book before heading off to the shops. It is not a big step to see how instinctive approaches to church life will not be too dissimilar to our shopping habits. The Church needs both instincts, and each has a great deal to learn from the other.

A recognition that all true mission is sharing in the *missio Dei* (mission of God) means that part of reviewing the situation must be spotting what God is already doing. The grave danger will be in slipping into assuming that if something is happening then it must be the work of God. Some churches and Christian groups are very adept at re-badging all current activity as mission, and a planning process that falls into this trap will end up with a plan that assumes the way forward is more of the same. Honest, prayerful planning, involving a range of voices, will be ready to look critically at cutting back current activities, and will need to do so if there is to be any space to see God doing something new. At the next stage, choosing future priorities cannot be answered with the simple response of 'Everything!' Time and human energy will not allow for that. Decisions have to be made, and so review needs to be challenging.

Tools for the job

Alongside a growing acceptance of the place of Mission Action Planning in setting church strategy, a range of tools have become increasingly well known, and dioceses have modified these in helpful ways that can also be accessed by others. One that is perhaps easily overlooked is the parish profile, which all Church of England parishes and groups have to go through the process of developing before a new minister can be sought. Once the new priest arrives, the parish profile may be filed and forgotten. This is a great loss. In compiling the profile the church, usually without significant input from clergy, has to work through how it sees itself and assess its hopes and dreams. Reviewing, reimagining and rewriting the profile once a minister has been in post for a few years can provide a valuable tool for taking stock, seeing the journey already made, and establishing aims for the future. Keeping an up-to-date profile also has the extra benefit of saving large amounts of time when a vacancy does occur, enabling a speedier appointment process.

Natural Church Development (NCD),[5] built on international research undertaken by Christian Schwarz and his team, provides a rigorous framework for measuring the health of different areas of church life. It takes a fair amount of time, money and effort – extensive questionnaires aim to gather data that are as objective as possible in revealing the strength of the eight key 'quality characteristics' of church life. They are:

Empowering	Leadership
Gift-based	Ministry
Passionate	Spirituality
Effective	Structures
Inspiring	Worship services
Holistic	Small groups
Need-oriented	Evangelism
Loving	Relationships

If the process seems long and complex, especially for the more active and intuitive members of the group, there is inspiration in focusing on the left-hand column in the list of quality characteristics. An empowering, gift-based, passionate, effective, inspiring, holistic, need-oriented and loving church is a pretty good place to be! More importantly, the next stage provides both affirmation and focus, since only the weakest quality characteristic, as revealed in the survey, need be given special attention. Many things in church life require only to be celebrated and continued, as specific areas for the focusing of new energy are identified.

The focus on church health is also found in other resources. Taking a similar approach, but with a lighter touch and an intuitive rather than a statistical basis, Healthy Churches, pioneered by Robert Warren, may be a more accessible starting point. The recently published *Developing Healthy Churches*[6] builds on Warren's earlier work, and gives both a rationale and practical instructions as to how the approach may be implemented. It contains a deeper focus on the essential spiritual nature of the task, with much of the material aiming to bring prayer and spirituality into the whole process. There is also a useful overview of how developing healthy churches can be woven together with the exercise of mission action planning.

As more parts of the Church nationally work to provide resources for Mission Action Planning, so a growing range of useful resources is becoming available for wider use. In particular, the Diocese of Liverpool's Growth Plan Framework[7] can be freely downloaded. Drawing on the insights of NCD and Healthy Churches, the framework will need modification and home-grown energy to put into action, but has a significant amount of valuable material that can be drawn upon by churches in other parts of the country.

Looking around

Used well, the tools outlined above will encourage those involved in pondering, listening and praying to look carefully at their own setting, the local area around and the people in it. What needs and opportunities do they see? How does the demographic and social profile of the congregation look when set alongside the whole surrounding population? Some will find themselves energized by grappling with Census data or other figures. Others will be itching to tell stories, to share the experiences of real people known to them. As different gifts and personalities play their part, so a fuller vision will emerge of what might be, and what needs to be done.

The challenge comes when a full and careful look at the local scene leads on to the question, 'So what might we do?' For some churches, deeply rooted in their local setting, feeling that they know the people around them, the instinctive answer may start with, 'Well, we always used to . . .' or 'I remember when . . .' And, of course, both may lead to valuable and fruitful strategies, but the grave danger is one of retrying old solutions, with the likelihood that this will lead to remembering why they didn't work last time! If there is to be fresh inspiration, it will probably be necessary to look beyond the regular congregation. This raises a number of possibilities, each with potential encouragements and potential challenges.

Big Christian gatherings and networks

Christians and churches have for a long time belonged to tribes. On the largest scale, denominations and the traditions within them – evangelical, liberal catholic, charismatic, for example – are relatively well known. For many churches and Christians, this belonging is reinforced by major gatherings and festivals when Christians of a similar spirituality and style meet together. New Wine draws around 30,000 people each summer, and the Greenbelt festival brings together around 10,000. While there will inevitably be difficulties in bringing back to local church life the experience of a huge gathering, each has the potential to provide spiritual challenge and inspiration. More than that, the main events, together with the year-round network of relationships they foster, provide a rich source of fresh thinking, and opportunities to take people outside the box of their own church and surroundings.

Bringing in ideas from big Christian gatherings will take careful handling, though, especially on the part of those overseeing the planning process. First, the stories that make their way into national events are likely to be pretty impressive – the organizers have an event to fill, after all – and most of local church life isn't. Scaling down, but holding on to important principles in what has been heard, may need wise local management. And second, national events draw those who choose to join in, and can generate their own powerful atmosphere. This can be true of other networks across the church spectrum, such as Affirming Catholicism, similarly reinforcing the convictions of the like-minded. What seems 'obvious' at New Wine may feel less so at Greenbelt, and may take time to communicate to a local church where not all share the exact theology or language of the national event. None of this diminishes the value of fresh thinking and valuable outside insights from national events, but it underlines the need for communication and adaptation before they can become embedded in the plans of many local congregations.

Branded or no logo?

Once an outside insight is seen, understood and welcomed, the next question to arise, and not only in Mission Action Planning but at any point in the mission of a local church, might be, 'Does the local church go with branding, or establish its own, distinctive but less well-known identity?'

Some brands are better known than others. Alpha has national recognition, and running an Alpha course under that name will attract some people who have encountered related logos or posters before. In a similar way, the red logo of Messy Church is now becoming fairly well recognized. That can draw people who have seen the image elsewhere and heard good things about it, and can be part of sharing the benefits of one local group with others. One leader of a thriving Messy Church explained:

> I have never attended a Messy Church 'How to do Messy Church' – and sort of worked out a pattern that would work for our context. So am I 'Messy Church'? We use the logo so that if a family moved, they could find something like it in their new area.

Other brands, for example Back to Church Sunday, have a lower profile and may not have the same impact. Or a local church may make a decision to be either more or less explicit about its own existing identity. 'Run by St George's Church' may add an important sense of rootedness and belonging to a new event. On the other hand, too strong a link may reduce the impact of a new enterprise or community that is working on a fresh venture.

Regardless of the brand, the key balancing decision is likely to be that between wider recognizability on the one hand and local distinctiveness with freedom to contextualize on the other. Quite apart from any concerns related to copyright, working with a well-known brand will emphasize shared identity with a wider movement, but going with a local name, colour scheme or logo will give more freedom to mark out what is distinctive, different and relevant to a specific setting.

Training, stories, welcoming outsiders and developing awareness

In our conversations and research through the course of writing, we have been powerfully impressed by the imagination, vision and energy of genuine pioneers. Sometimes we have simply listened awestruck as people have told us their stories. But those occasions have been relatively few. More often, the way forward for the rest of us who are not exceptional innovators will be to borrow and adapt what others are already doing.

The process of planning needs wise, prayerful reflection upon the current situation. It should certainly also be open to the spontaneous, off-the-wall and imaginative. But if there is to be thinking outside the current box, fresh inspiration and ideas may be required from elsewhere. Even some of the resources explored above, working with church health, for example, may serve mainly to encourage fresh thinking about how to reach out from the existing base. Really radical thinking, for example establishing a café church or Messy Church, will seldom emerge purely on the basis of local reflection. Training courses such as those run by Leading your Church into Growth[8] can broaden horizons and open up new possibilities.

Often, though, fresh thinking may be closer to home. Working with an observer from a neighbouring church can open up possibilities of seeing things differently. Observers from right outside the church, including people of other faiths and none, may offer new insights in their comments and ideas. They may not always be easy to respond to, but at the very least the reality of how others view us will colour the plans that follow. This may be the place where the community will need to be ready to listen to those with prophetic instincts and a particular openness to God. Prophets do not sit easily within a measured planning process, and they may be people who initially throw everything off course, but then oblige everybody to stop, ponder and recognize that perhaps the voice of God has been heard.

From Plan to action

Once the planning process is completed, there needs to be a plan. This may seem an unnecessary statement, but it marks a significant move. The phase of thinking, reviewing and devising is coming to an end, and from it all specific outcomes need to be formulated. Choices have to be made, a plan agreed and action to follow.

Plans cannot include the unachievable. That is not to give up on vision, but to recognize that planned steps need actually to be practically possible. Frequently, the language of SMART targets is used:

Specific
Measurable
Achievable
Realistic
Time Bound

The great value of SMART targets is that they have a reasonable chance of being hit, and it will be clear when they have not. Churches show great expertise, developed over many years, in reinterpreting failure as success, as in: 'The rain at the fete meant only one lady and a dog attended, but the dog did indeed seem blessed by the experience.' SMART targets make that harder to do.

That will lead on to the next, vital part of the process: review. If a MAP has been adopted, has it led to the actions anticipated in the time frame planned? The likelihood is that the answer will be 'Well, yes, partly', but the part should have been identified for that answer to be given. Review can in turn lead on to celebration, thanking God for what has emerged, and then starting the next phase in developing a fresh plan.

Sticking to the MAP regardless?

Some years ago, walking in the Brecon Beacons with my son, I found myself growing increasingly puzzled as to exactly where we were. The landmarks seemed to be there, but we were not encountering them in the right order, and the landscape just didn't look quite as we expected it to. Eventually we realized we were climbing up a different spur, parallel to the one we thought we were on. Fortunately, once that was spotted it was easy to chart a new course from that point, but we had to stop and recognize the reality of our situation. It was only when we admitted that we had made a mistake that we could move forward confidently. Similarly, a MAP needs to be followed with eyes open. It can't be treated like carelessly used satnav, taking us where we need to go without us really understanding the route or our current location. Wise use of a MAP will involve a combination of sticking to course and acknowledging the need for change.

From kerb drill to the Green Cross Code

Older readers, if they were brought up in the UK, will almost certainly remember the simple, clear road safety message summed up in the 'kerb drill'. In the memorable, and wonderfully militaristic phrase: 'At the kerb, halt. Look right, look left, look right again – if all clear, quick march!'

Children growing up in the 1960s were well trained in checking the road before crossing. Even so, when one of my friends followed the drill and did just that, he was unfortunately killed by an unseen car appearing suddenly around a corner.

The Green Cross Code appeared in 1970, and continues in modified form. Rather more complicated, the message was that crossing a road is something that needs ongoing attention. The last phrase, 'keep looking and listening', might have saved my friend's life.

A MAP, if followed blindly once initial plans are agreed, can be as limiting as the old-style kerb drill. Keep looking and listening, watch for surprises and unexpected changes – these need to be part of life once the initial aims in a MAP are agreed.

Holding to the course

One value of a MAP is that it sets out a clear, shared commitment to movement in a certain direction. This can be of considerable significance when a new venture has a slow start, and a whole church may need to be reminded of this shared commitment until support grows and it becomes a reality. Particularly where major financial resources are required, it can take time for everyone in the church to grasp the scale of the challenge, and the possibility of rising to it. Initial pledges and gifts may be disappointing; encouragement, sharing stories of where similar projects have succeeded elsewhere, and concerted prayer that people will indeed start to give will all have their part. The beginning may be slow, but the firm commitment to action allows for pressing on in the face of early disappointment.

In many other cases, a relatively familiar pattern is encountered. Initial enthusiasm can be followed by a trough, as the reality of long-term commitment sinks in. What has started brightly may, after a while, appear to have been a flash in the pan. This is not unique to local church life, and closely follows what has become known as the Gartner Hype Cycle. The graph in Figure 3.2 draws on research into the adoption of new technologies. The precise details of its validity have been much debated in the business world, but it can be highly relevant to the newly adopted elements of a MAP.

Early success can inflate hopes about a new direction in church life – for example, as dozens of retired people attend a holiday

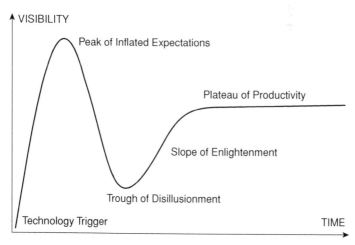

Figure 3.2 The Hype Cycle[9]

event or two new Pilgrim groups start up. This parallels the hype seen in the business world around the potential of some new technologies. As we have noted previously when looking at the Alpha course,[10] the test of long-term effectiveness may be a willingness to hang on in there through the trough of disillusionment, as initial high attendance is followed by times when it is hard to attract the same numbers of people to the course. Although honest assessment once the period of a MAP has finished and the review process begins may lead to the conclusion that the venture concerned has not been a success, the care put into the planning process will mean that premature abandonment is less likely to be seen as an option.

Keeping our eyes open

As the Hype Cycle graph suggests, moving from disillusionment to productivity does not happen automatically. There is a slope of enlightenment, as fresh insights are brought to bear. This is exactly where the personalities of those who struggle with an over-mechanistic approach can flourish. There is a need to keep looking and listening, to see whether or not the original starting direction was exactly right, or whether the world around is changing and adjustments need to be made in the light of fresh circumstances.

In the case of Alpha, our earlier study found that initial, high attendance was often made up of interested church members. The smaller numbers attending successive courses were actually more likely to be enquirers, possibly leading to genuine church growth. Here the need was for a deeper understanding of what was going on, not for a change of course.

In other settings, continued listening to God and to the world around has pointed to the need to make adjustments. A few years ago, an urban church in Cambridge started a Saturday community lunch, open to all-comers. It soon outgrew the capacity of those running it, becoming a victim of its own success, and was drawing more homeless people than could easily be managed. After discussion between regular members and those providing the lunch, the decision was made to move from Saturday lunch to Sunday afternoon tea. The welcome was by invitation, although in reality all were invited, and the quality of listening, support and spiritual encouragement was recognized as the focus, rather than quantity in terms of people or of food.

Starting with God's surprises

So far our consideration of the balance between strategy and spontaneity has focused mainly on Mission Action Planning. While good planning will look very hard at what God is already doing, the initiative behind the whole process is still a human one. At other times, God's surprises will set the agenda; the important thing is to spot this, and catch up with God.

Very frequently, life will start with death. A congregation or group that dies of old age will leave the survivors facing the prospect of starting out in a new direction. For one inner suburban congregation in Cambridge, the dwindling, ageing congregation recognized the need for a fresh start if there was to be any hope for the future. Working with a large nearby church of similar theology but very different style, they had the courage to welcome a church graft. Forty new members joined them, along with a new incumbent as he finished his curacy and moved with the group to become the new vicar. The change was challenging, but the growth that has followed has been remarkable.

Most often it is buildings that die. For good or ill, buildings exercise a powerful hold on those who worship in them. The instinct of the church members will usually be weighted towards seeking new ways of using and restoring existing buildings. It may be asbestos or roof collapse that finally open eyes to God's new possibilities. The story of St Luke's in the High Street, Walthamstow, provides an especially striking example, but it is only one among many.

Donna Gwilliams is church warden at St Luke's. Born in Walthamstow and baptized at the church, she remembers the beginning of a prayerful discernment process around 2000 when the District Church Council (DCC) started to discuss where God might be leading. 'We knew we had to make some serious decisions,' she says. 'We had a strong vision to reach the High Street – but we realized we were apart from the centre, that the mission heart wasn't in the right place.'

Their building was another problem and urgently needed investment. While it was a good space for youth activities, as a place of worship it was cold and unwelcoming. Donna says: 'When I took over as church warden, I inherited a big, cold and draughty building, a leaking roof and lots of buckets – needed to collect the drips. As regulars, we were thinking, we don't really want to be here; why should anyone else want to come?'

The combination of a longing for more effective outreach to the high street with the burden of an ageing building focused minds. Then the possibility arose to link up with London Farmers' Market, which was looking to open a centre of operations in Walthamstow. So the courageous decision was made to become a church that had left its building behind. The visible presence was a market stall. St Luke's in the High Street was born, worshipping midweek in homes and a hired hall and using the opportunity of the market to run a welcome for tired shoppers, the homeless and others met on the high street.

God's circumstances, people with open eyes and the support of a team ministry that was ready to see God at work in new ways, allowed St Luke's to become a church without a building, but present on the high street where God's call had been heard.[11]

Perhaps a fundamental lesson is that churches are best able to respond to the unexpected when the regular and expected are done well. They are able to act with agility when the planning is careful, and the people understand the underlying vision that motivates all that happens. In keeping this vision central, new shoots will be able to spring up in what is already healthy ground.

4

Jesus requests the pleasure ...

———◆·◆·◆———

You Europeans have the watches, we have the time.
(The words of a Pakistani friend when I was
teaching in northern Pakistan as a young graduate)

In this chapter we want to pause, to take a step back from thinking about practical considerations and strategies, and look at the Gospels, to see what we can learn for our own situation from how Jesus went about making disciples in the very different world of the first century.

Time for one-to-one conversations

One of the paradoxes we face is that we live in a society with more electronic gadgets and 'time-saving' devices than ever before, and yet we constantly feel short of time and under pressure to do several things at once. We are in danger of losing the ability to sit still and listen to others who need our attention, without feeling compelled to do something else at the same time – even though, of course, we have all had the frustration of trying to talk to someone who isn't fully listening. Christian leaders can be especially prone to the temptation to be busy and multi-task, perhaps scanning emails while we listen to someone on the phone. It may be that because of the importance of the gospel we feel somehow driven, in the words of Kipling, 'to fill the unforgiving minute with sixty seconds of distance run'.

Given the pressures we face, what can we learn from the life of Jesus, recorded in the Gospels? Jesus clearly took time to listen to individuals, as well as teaching large groups in the synagogue and the open air. Allowing for various overlaps between the Gospels, we seem to have around 29 recorded conversations of Jesus talking to individuals – see Table 4.1. In the last chapter we argued that the best way to grow the Church is to focus on growing people, and that churches that want to grow people need to give attention not only to preaching and small groups but also to fostering one-to-one mentoring or discipling relationships. In this chapter we want to see what we can learn from Jesus' example. Even though he had a world to save, and only two or three brief years of public ministry, Jesus gave a lot of time to one-to-one encounters with those who were not already part of his community of disciples. He was drawing large crowds, and had teams at his command (the 12, the 72), yet he clearly didn't decide to concentrate on the big speaking opportunities and leave his disciples to do the personal inviting and follow-up.

How busy was Jesus?

In Mark's Gospel Jesus appears to be very busy. There is a certain breathless quality about the narrative in the early chapters, underlined by his repeated use of the Greek word *euthus* (translated 'immediately' or 'straight away'), which occurs over 40 times in the Gospel – including 11 times in the first chapter.[1] As Mark depicts 'a day in the life of Jesus' in 1.21–35 he is always rushing on to the next thing, and twice (in 3.20 and 6.30) we read that the gathering crowds meant that he didn't even have time to eat.

However, the beginning of Jesus' ministry feels very different in the Fourth Gospel. In John 1 Jesus' approach seems laid-back and relational; when two of John's disciples start following him and ask where he lives, he says simply, 'Come and see,' and they spend the rest of the day together. The next day he decides to set off for Galilee and invites someone else from Bethsaida, Philip, to come on the hike; Philip in turn finds his friend Nathaniel; the day after that they end up in Cana and join the guests at a family wedding. Jesus' approach to discipleship in these chapters can be summed up as sharing life, and inviting people on a journey.

48

Table 4.1 Conversations with Jesus in the Gospels[2]

1	Simon and Andrew	Matthew 4.18–20; Mark 1.16–18; Luke 5.1–11; John 1.35–43
2	A man suffering with leprosy	Matthew 8.1–4; Mark 1.40–45; Luke 5.12–16
3	The centurion	Matthew 8.5–13; Luke 7.1–10
4	A paralysed man	Matthew 9.1–8; Mark 2.1–12; Luke 5.17–19
5	The calling of Matthew/Levi	Matthew 9.9–13; Mark 2.13–17; Luke 5.27–32
6	Two blind men	Matthew 9.27–31
7	The man with the withered hand	Matthew 12.9–14; Mark 3.1–6; Luke 6.6–11
8	The widow of Nain	Luke 7.11–17
9	The woman with the alabaster jar of ointment	Luke 7.36–50
10	The Gerasene demoniac	Mark 5.1–20; Luke 8.26–39
11	Jairus' daughter and the woman with haemorrhages	Mark 5.21–43; Luke 8.40–56
12	The Syro-Phoenician woman	Matthew 15.21–28; Mark 7.24–30
13	The blind man of Bethsaida	Mark 8.22–26
14	The father of the epileptic boy	Matthew 17.14–19; Mark 9.14–29; Luke 9.37–45
15	The lawyer	Matthew 22.34–40; Mark 12.28–31; Luke 10.25–37
16	The man in the crowd	Luke 12.13–21
17	The woman with a spirit of infirmity	Luke 13.10–17
18	Ten men suffering with leprosy	Luke 17.11–19
19	The rich young ruler	Matthew 19.16–30; Mark 10.17–31; Luke 18.18–30
20	Zacchaeus	Luke 19.1–10
21	Philip and Nathaniel	John 1.43–51
22	Nicodemus	John 3.1–16
24	The woman at the well	John 4.1–42
25	The royal official with a sick son	John 4.43–54
26	The disabled man at the pool of Bethesda	John 5.1–15
27	The woman caught in adultery	John 8.1–11
28	The man born blind	John 9.1–41
29	Mary and Martha	John 11.1–46

In John's Gospel Jesus has lengthy conversations in a single setting, for example with Nicodemus in chapter 3 and the woman at the well in chapter 4. Regarding Jesus' encounter with the Samaritan woman, in his book *Working from a Place of Rest*, Tony Horsfall makes the significant observation that 'everything that happens in this story happens because Jesus was doing nothing'. Tired from his journey he sat down to rest by a well, and was happy for the disciples to go off to get food. It was because he was doing nothing that he had time to chat to the Samaritan woman, and out of that unplanned conversation not only is her life transformed but the whole Samaritan town experiences revival. Horsfall's exposition of this passage leads him to affirm:

> We can learn to work and minister as Jesus did, from a place of rest. Christian ministry need not be a matter of striving to make things happen or of straining to achieve our goals through the sweat of our brow. We can learn to work together with God just as Jesus did, for this was no idle moment; rather it was a moment of communion, of sensing what the Father was doing and of responding accordingly ... If we slow down and take time to listen, he will guide us so that we can share in what he is doing.[3]

The Fourth Gospel shows us a Jesus who himself is constantly listening to the Father, who only does what he sees the Father doing. 'I do nothing on my own, but I speak these things as the Father instructed me' (John 8.28). 'What I speak, therefore, I speak just as the Father has told me' (12.50).

How is it that the pace of Jesus' ministry feels so different through the eyes of two different Gospel writers? Perhaps our own life stage and experience influence how we see Jesus. If Mark was perhaps only a teenager at the time of Jesus' crucifixion, and was writing the first Gospel around AD 60, he could have been writing in his early forties. Whereas if the Fourth Gospel was written much later and relies substantially on the testimony of the apostle John, those stories could well have been written down when John was in his seventies. If two evangelists, both inspired by God, can see the ministry of Jesus so differently, we should not worry if some criticize us for being too busy while others criticize us for not doing enough and spending too much time on a few individuals who aren't important (at least in the eyes of our critics).

Engagement and withdrawal

The challenge is how, on the one hand, to have real spiritual depth in the middle of busy lives and, on the other hand, to be godly and contemplative people who actually get things done. In his seminal book *The Contemplative Pastor*, Eugene Peterson declares provocatively that pastors are busy for one of only two reasons: either because they are vain – they like to feel important, rushing from one thing to the next – or because they are lazy, allowing other people to write their job descriptions and dump all sorts of extraneous responsibilities on them. Peterson argues that the proper role of a pastor is not to allow his or her time to be used up 'running' the church (which lay leaders may be far better at), but instead to be a pastor who prays, a pastor who preaches and a pastor who listens.[4]

Having said that, Peterson's experience of being a pastor was in the USA, and didn't include maintaining half a dozen crumbling ancient buildings with tiny elderly congregations that lack gifts in organization and leadership! At a time when management and organizational thinking seem to be ever more highly prized in growing the Church, Peterson's insights remind us that these three themes of prayer, preaching and listening lie at the heart of Jesus' approach to making disciples, and need to inspire our strategy too.

Even in Mark's busy narrative, Jesus makes deliberate time for rest and withdrawal, and for being with his Father. After a hectic night of ministry in 1.32–34, Jesus gets up very early in the morning and goes off to a solitary place to pray. And when the disciples track him down (literally 'hunt him down', a very strong phrase) and tell him, 'Everyone is looking for you!', he simply replies, 'Let's go somewhere else.' Later, in 6.31, Jesus says to the disciples, 'Come away to a deserted place all by yourselves and rest a while.' Further on in the same chapter, after the arrival of the 5,000 has led to another time of extensive ministry, Jesus makes the disciples set off in the boat so that he can have time alone to pray (6.45–46). In the ministry of Jesus, while discipling others includes time for individuals and time for the crowd, it doesn't mean being endlessly available: he guards time alone, even to the point of apparently disappearing to a house in Tyre (beyond the borders of Israel) and not wanting anyone to know he was there (7.24 – a verse, incidentally, which has always given me permission not to answer the door or the phone on my day off!).

Strategic or spontaneous?

As well as the examples of spontaneity noted above, there are indications in the Gospels of Jesus having a clear plan and priorities. Jesus' decision to move from Nazareth, an isolated community in the hills where he had been brought up, to Capernaum, a bustling lakeside port, commercial centre and border post close to a major trade route, the Via Maris, would have immediately brought his ministry to much wider notice. And although he was based in the region known since the days of Isaiah the prophet as 'Galilee of the Gentiles' (Matthew 4.15), Jesus clearly focused his attention on the Jews. In his encounter with the Syro-Phoenician woman (Matthew 15.21–28; Mark 7.24–30), Jesus seems reluctant to heal her daughter. He answers, 'I was sent only to the lost sheep of the house of Israel,' indicating that the focus of his short ministry was only on Israel, leaving the Gentile mission to be carried out by the apostles after the resurrection. However, although he has a clear plan, he is still willing to make exceptions on the spur of the moment, as when moved by this Gentile woman's great faith.[5]

In Mark 6.6–13 and parallels we see Jesus employing a clear discipling strategy, as he sends out the 12 disciples in pairs; having watched his ministry at close quarters, it was now their turn to go and preach and heal themselves. Roger Walton points out just how little actual teaching the disciples had received from Jesus before they were sent out on their first mission. 'Despite the thin teaching content up to this point, Jesus sends his disciples on a mission where they do what they have seen Jesus doing: proclaim the kingdom, heal the sick and cast out demons.'[6]

The first mission trip is followed by Peter's confession and the Transfiguration, after which comes a clear strategic decision and literal change of direction, which forms the turning point of the Gospels: 'When the days drew near for him to be taken up, he set his face to go to Jerusalem' (Luke 9.51). As Jesus embarks on the road to Jerusalem he begins to teach the disciples more, but even then the teaching often arises out of the situations they encounter, and as they travel he also sends out the 72 ahead of him to the places he was about to go (Luke 10.1).

As we have seen, in the Gospels disciples are formed not by classroom learning but by spending time with Jesus and by being sent out. The way Jesus trains his disciples has clear implications for how we equip people for ministry today – which we shall explore in Chapter 12.

Meeting people in everyday life

Visiting the Sea of Galilee recently, I saw the so-called 'Jesus boat', a wooden vessel discovered embedded in the mud of the lake floor a few years ago, when drought had made the water level exceptionally low. The boat is of a size suitable for fishing, and dates from the first century, hence the nickname. One remarkable feature of the boat, archaeologists discovered, was that 12 different types of wood were used in its construction, a number of them clearly reused from other vessels or objects. Pondering the skills needed to build and repair boats like that made me realize that carpenters and fishermen in a place like Capernaum would naturally have known each other and worked together, which suggests that the encounter on the shore would not have been their first meeting, and may explain Peter's apparent willingness to let Jesus commandeer his boat as a pulpit in Luke 5.3.

The call of the first disciples happened at their place of work, when Simon and Andrew were casting their net into the sea, and James and John were mending their nets. Matthew's encounter with Jesus also happened at his place of work, which challenges us to think about how well our churches equip people to be disciples when dispersed in their daily life and places of work. Tracey Cotterell and Neil Hudson make the point that of the 168 hours in a week, people are usually awake for around 120, and out of these in reality most church members will not spend more than ten hours at church and church activities.

> So 110 hours will be spent elsewhere – largely at home, work or in the neighbourhood. This is their primary mission field for witness and service, and the primary context of their discipleship for God's work of forming Christ in them.[7]

If that is so, how well do these ten hours equip people to live as disciples in the 110, on their own personal front line, at home, work, sport or other responsibilities? Is that really the focus of our preaching and teaching, our home groups and church meetings, or is the discipleship training we offer actually forming disciples to take on more responsibility in church, in ministries the gathered church thinks are important?

Special concern for those on the edge

When one examines the list of Jesus' conversations with individuals (see Table 4.1), it is clear that he is particularly careful to give time and attention to those considered by the disciples or the crowd as not important (children, the woman with the issue of blood, the blind beggar Bartimaeus, the Samaritan leper) and to those judged or looked down on by others (the Samaritan woman at the well, the rich tax collector Zacchaeus, the woman caught in adultery). Jesus is criticized because he 'welcomes sinners and eats with them' and is accused of being a drunkard because he is friendly towards tax collectors and sinners (Luke 7.34). The Pharisees, being the most religious people of the day, clearly expected that he should spend most of his time with them, whereas Jesus replies, 'Those who are well have no need of a physician, but those who are sick; I have come to call not the righteous but sinners' (Mark 2.17).

Jesus' concern for those looked down on by others is seen in the way he is willing to keep the desperate – and highly influential – synagogue ruler waiting while he seeks out the unclean woman who touched the hem of his garment. This woman would have been excluded from the synagogue because of her condition, and yet the ruler of the synagogue is made to wait until she has heard Jesus' word of peace and had her healing confirmed among her community (Luke 8.48). Jairus might have been angered by the delay in Jesus' arrival at his house, and by the fact that he had been made unclean on the way by a defiled woman touching him. However, perhaps seeing the dignity Jesus bestowed on the woman was a significant step in his own discipleship, alongside the eventual raising of his daughter to life. If so, then by following Jesus' example in the care and respect we accord to clients at foodbanks, to asylum seekers and to rough sleepers in our churchyards, we may help others glimpse the Lord we serve.

No set formula

When reading Jesus' conversations inviting people to follow him, it is clear that he does not have a set approach, or seek to communicate a standard message, or evoke a set way of responding. This contrasts in our minds with the excellent training in how to give an evangelistic talk which we (the authors) both received when leading summer house parties for teenagers, where the essentials to be included in the message before the invitation was given were clearly spelled out. Those of other traditions might not feel comfortable with this kind of set approach, but we probably all have our own summary of what the essential message is. Presumably Jesus did too, but he does not seem to have imposed it.

There is no 'one size fits all' approach to welcome or discipling in the Gospels. Rather than following a set procedure, or explaining certain key propositions, Jesus seeks to develop a relationship within which he discerns what the specific next step might be that each individual needs to take if he or she truly wants to follow him. Sometimes there seems to be no challenge at all – the grace Jesus offers takes the form of simple gift, responding in compassion to a human need without asking anything in return, for example when he encounters a funeral procession and raises the widow of Nain's son to life (Luke 7.11–17). When the man with the withered hand is set up by some Pharisees as a test to see if he would heal on the Sabbath, Jesus is both angry and deeply grieved at the man's treatment, and proceeds to heal his hand, but he makes no demands on his life and does not invite him to follow. It appears to be a very costly encounter for Jesus, provoking the first plots to take his life, but Jesus seeks nothing in return (Mark 3.1–6).

The open and undemanding nature of some encounters contrasts with other occasions where Jesus appears to set the bar very high. Simon and Andrew are challenged to surrender their fishing business and become fishers of people at the very moment when trade was booming after a miraculous catch of fish, just when they could probably afford to expand. When the rich young ruler who has led a morally upright life comes to Jesus anxious to gain eternal life, Jesus loves him and says to him, 'You lack one thing; go, sell what you own, and give the money to the poor, and you will have treasure in heaven; then come, follow me' (Mark 10.21). Jesus loves him enough to put his finger on the one thing in his life that is holding him back from wholehearted discipleship.

Amendment of life

It is interesting to note when Jesus does and doesn't refer to sin in his encounters. When the paralysed man is brought to Jesus by his four friends, they are simply seeking physical healing, but Jesus brings up the subject of sin – he sees a deeper need and gives the man something more: 'Son, your sins are forgiven' (Mark 2.5). In contrast, in John 9.3 he clearly refutes any link between sin and disease in the case of the man born blind. When Jesus encounters tax collectors, regarded as sinners almost by definition in first-century Palestine, he doesn't bring up the subject. To Levi he says simply, 'Follow me,' and Levi leaves everything behind. The first mention of sin in the story is when the Pharisees criticize Jesus for eating with tax collectors and sinners and Jesus replies, 'I have come to call not the righteous but sinners' (Mark 2.17). Similarly, Luke suggests that when Jesus encounters Zacchaeus he begins the relationship by talking not about sin but about supper (Luke 19.5).

This chimes with my own experience. In my second curacy I was also chaplain of HM Prison Lancaster, a forbidding medieval castle where my chapel was high up in the Norman keep. During my time there I saw several men come to repentance, faith and new life in Christ. I didn't have to tell them they were sinners – they knew that already. What they needed to hear was that there is a Saviour from sin, and that his name is Jesus.

Jesus was not shy of talking about sin to those who thought they were righteous – to the scribes and Pharisees, whom he called whitewashed tombs (Matthew 23.27) – but to those who knew their lives were in a mess his words were words of hope not condemnation. When a sinful woman anoints Jesus' feet in the home of a Pharisee, Jesus interprets her costly act of love as a sign that her sins have been forgiven; he assures her, 'Your sins are forgiven . . . Your faith has saved you' (Luke 7.48, 50). Here Jesus' challenge is to the behaviour of the Pharisee, not the woman, who is given no instruction but to 'go in peace'.

Sometimes Jesus directs people as to what to do after the encounter (to show themselves to the chief priest, or to keep the healing secret); where he does so, people sometimes obey him and sometimes they do the opposite, as when the man healed of leprosy spread the news far and wide and Jesus was unable to enter a town openly (Mark 1.45).

When we read Jesus' conversations in the first three Gospels, they seem to be 'brief encounters' or one-offs, but in John there are indications that at least some healings were part of a longer process of discipling or mentoring, with Jesus following up a previous contact. For example, the man Jesus healed at the pool of Bethesda had no idea who Jesus was, until Jesus found him later in the day in the temple and told him to stop sinning, lest something worse than illness might happen to him (John 5.13–15). The account of Jesus healing the man born blind in John 9 indicates stages in his faith journey: when he is healed he only knows his name (9.11); later he affirms that he is a prophet (9.17); then he identifies him as a godly man sent by God (9.31–33); and when he is thrown out of the synagogue Jesus goes looking for him and reveals himself as the Son of God, at which point the man declares his belief and worships Jesus.

Not giving answers but asking questions

Jesus engages the curiosity of those who are seeking by telling stories and by asking questions rather than answering them – it has been calculated that in the Gospels he is asked 183 questions and answers just three of them – and he asks 307 questions back! As Don Everts and Doug Schaupp comment, 'Jesus doesn't have Q&A sessions, he has Q&Q sessions!'[8]

For example, when a lawyer asks Jesus just the question we as evangelists would all love to ask, 'What must I do to inherit eternal life?' (Luke 10.25), Jesus doesn't launch into an answer but instead asks him two questions. When the man answers correctly but comes up with another question, Jesus replies by telling a story and then asks a further question (10.36). And when he is asked to intervene in a property dispute, Jesus replies with a question, and then tells a story that ends with a question on the lips of God himself (Luke 12.13–21).

Whereas evangelism has too often been caricatured as offering answers to questions no one is asking, part of the genius of Alpha has been the use of small groups in which guests are encouraged to 'ask anything'. How can we arouse curiosity in Jesus? By following his example in asking the right kind of questions to get people thinking about the most important things. We shall be thinking further about Alpha and other courses in Chapters 6 and 7. Likewise, there is a messiness or untidiness about Jesus' approach, so if Messy Church doesn't give all the answers, maybe that's all right – we will explore this further in Chapter 9.

Not afraid to disappoint

Jesus is happy to debate, but he is also not afraid to disappoint. Reading the Gospels there are clearly times when he disappointed the expectations of the crowds and even of his disciples. In Mark 1.37, when the disciples finally track down Jesus, they clearly think he should go back and satisfy the crowd, whereas he, fresh from time alone with his Father, is free from feeling the need to meet those expectations, and instead leads them on to nearby villages to preach there. Straight after Peter's confession Jesus has to disabuse him of his wrong ideas of the kind of Messiah that he was hoping for (Mark 8.31–33). It seems that Jesus doesn't really meet John the Baptist's preconceptions of what the Messiah should do either, causing him to send messengers to ask, 'Are you the one who is to come, or are we to wait for another?' (Matthew 11.3). Learning that we may have to disappoint those closest to us in ministry in order not to disappoint our heavenly Father is a hard but liberating lesson in our own growth as disciples.

Who are the people Jesus doesn't engage with?

Having reflected on what we can learn from Jesus' conversations with individuals in the Gospels, it is worth pausing for a moment to consider the kinds of people Jesus doesn't converse with. Over my 30 years as a priest I have paid too much attention to the words of those who would flatter me with their expectations, and also those who would mock me or accuse me unfairly. Jesus does not engage with people who wanted to make him king by force – he simply withdraws himself (John 6.15). In John 8.48 he is accused of both being a Samaritan and having a demon – a huge double insult in that culture – but he does not waste energy answering the charges. Where there is evidence of serious enquiry Jesus gives time, but when there is just nastiness, he ignores it. Nor does he defend himself against the false accusations put to him by the high priest and Pilate in the Sanhedrin (Mark 14.61; Matthew 27.14) – he remains silent. Being sure of our own calling and confident of the Father's approval enables us to be not diverted either by those who flatter us for their own ends, or by those who would accuse us.

Conclusion

In seeking to learn from Jesus we also have to be honest and admit that we aren't Jesus – so we need to be aware of the limits of our wisdom and the dangers of misusing power in any discipling relationship. That is why, in a culture that has painfully learned that those in positions of trust are not always trustworthy, models of discipling that are mutual – holding one another to account – are likely to be healthier and safer than any top-down or hierarchical approach to discipling or 'shepherding'.

Space has not allowed us to explore the place of the demonic or of spiritual warfare in Jesus' encounters in the Gospels. That is a specialist area that lies beyond the scope of this book. Nor has space allowed us to explore the examples of faith-sharing in Acts and the epistles.

However, in examining the different ways Jesus invites people to be his disciples recorded in the Gospels, we have seen not only that he begins each conversation differently, but that conversations also end differently. It is not that Jesus begins in a different place and seeks to bring each individual to the same point; rather, the journey of each disciple is different. What Jesus demands of one he does not necessarily demand of another. Like Peter we are tempted to look over our shoulder and see if someone else's journey with Jesus might be easier – or more exciting – than our own. Like Peter we each need to hear Jesus' personal call to us, 'What is that to you? Follow me!' (John 21.22).

5

God's work or ours? Praying for new disciples and spiritual growth

————•◦•————

> There is no example of the renewal of the church in the West that does not begin with a renewal of prayer and religious communities.
>
> (Archbishop Justin Welby)

In his first presidential address as Archbishop of Canterbury, Justin Welby outlined his three personal priorities: prayer and the renewal of the religious life, reconciliation, and evangelism and witness. About prayer he said:

> If we want to see things changed, it starts with prayer. It starts with a new spirit of prayer, using all the traditions, ancient and modern. When it comes, it will be linked to what has gone before, but it will look different – because it is a new renewal for new times. God's created community is perfectly designed for its time and place. It almost always comes from below. It comes from Christians seeking Christ.

As part of his commitment to the renewal of the religious life, one of Welby's first acts as archbishop was to invite members of the ecumenical Chemin Neuf community to base themselves at Lambeth Palace and share with him the daily round of prayer. He has also initiated a new religious community of young people, the Community of St Anselm, also based at Lambeth Palace and sharing a common life of prayer, study and service to the poor.

Prayer and renewal in history

There are a number of examples from history of the renewal of the Church beginning with prayer. In the third century Anthony the Great heard the call of Christ as a young man and went out into the desert to devote himself to prayer, ultimately spending the last decades of his life in a cave in the wilderness. It must have seemed to his contemporaries such a waste of talent, wealth and opportunity, yet with him began a tradition of desert spirituality that has been an immense gift to the wider Church and later inspired Benedict's Rule. Today, the monasteries of the Coptic Church in Egypt are seeing a remarkable renewal of religious life and growth in numbers in the midst of struggle and persecution.

The evangelization of Britain owes much to monasticism. The Celtic monks of Iona and Lindisfarne were the early evangelists of northern Britain, while southern Britain was evangelized by a band of monks from Rome led by their prior, Augustine. The Rule of St Benedict spread a moderate religious life through the Western Church in the early middle ages, providing stable centres of spirituality and prayer amid the turbulence, violence and corruption of both Church and state. The founding of a monastery at Cluny in the tenth century stimulated a widespread renewal of religious life and the suppression of worldliness and corruption. Francis and Dominic renewed the Church in the thirteenth century through mendicant orders dedicated to prayer, poverty and preaching.

However, the Church has not always been good at spotting new things the Spirit is doing and welcoming renewal. In 1215 the Fourth Lateran Council placed a ban on the formation of new religious orders, which historians identify as a factor in the rise of late medieval heresy, as those with spiritual fervour who were appalled by the torpor of organized religion increasingly looked outside the Church for ways to express their spirituality. The Franciscan friars squeezed in under the wire – Francis only managed to get his new order recognized by borrowing an existing Rule – but the inflexibility of the late medieval Church towards the spiritual zeal of the Lollards and the Hussites meant that they were condemned as heretics, and this contributed to the fracture of the Western Church.

The English Reformation was a season of renewal in the life of the Church, which was preceded not by reform of the religious life but by the plundering and dissolution of the monasteries – in so doing suppressing a form of religious life that did not reappear in the Church of England for three centuries. However, a key factor in the English Reformation was the printing and circulation of the Bible in English; previously this had been illegal and copies were smuggled in from the Continent and spread secretly from house to house. Reading the preface to the Book of Common Prayer, it seems that Cranmer hoped and intended that local parish churches should become the places where local communities gathered daily to say the offices, summoned by the priest tolling the bell, but as far as we know this vision never really took off. Rather, the home became the centre of daily prayer and religious instruction, as families gathered each day around the printed family Bible, to read the Scriptures in their own language.

In the eighteenth century it was the Holy Club in Oxford and people in small groups (classes and bands) devoted to personal transformation that were the wellspring of the Methodist revival. However, Wesley's much admired class meetings actually began for a very different purpose, originating as a means to pay off the loan on the Bristol Methodist building by collecting a penny a week from each of 12 members! Wesley soon realized, though, that this model of a small group in touch with a leader every week was an effective form of pastoral oversight and support for the poor against backsliding into drunkenness and violence.

With the benefit of hindsight we can see that this Evangelical Revival was another example of the established Church failing to recognize a new move of the Spirit, fearful as it was of the dangers of 'enthusiasm' after the bloody conflict between Puritans and Royalists in the seventeenth century. This inflexibility squeezed Wesley's followers out of the Church of England, forcing them to form a new church – Methodism – rather than participate – with other Anglicans like Henry Venn of Huddersfield – in the renewal of the old. How different discipleship might have looked in the Church of England if Wesley's genius for organizing worshippers in classes and bands had been harnessed rather than rejected.

The growth of Protestant individualism, centred on family prayers and personal 'quiet time' rather than on religious communities or the parish church, proved a very effective channel for passing on the Christian faith to succeeding generations, but something important was lost in the process. In the Church of England – in contrast to the Church of Scotland, for example – missionary endeavour became 'privatized', passed on to para-church organizations such as the British and Foreign Bible Society, the Church Missionary Society and the Church Pastoral Aid Society, rather than undertaken by the Church itself. Much has been achieved by such agencies, but this may have had an unintended consequence for ecclesiology, in that the parts of the Church most concerned for evangelism were those with the weakest theology of the Church: 'What matters is your walk with the Lord – don't worry too much about the church.'

The renewal of the religious life today

In the light of history, any strategy for making new disciples and re-evangelizing our nation would do well to begin by seeking the renewal of the religious life and the forming of new religious communities. Membership of traditional religious orders in England, both Anglican and Roman Catholic, has been in decline for many years. Similarly, the weekly whole church prayer meeting, once such a feature of evangelical parishes, is now a rarity, supported by a few faithful diehards. And the home is no longer the centre of prayer and religious instruction it once was. According to research by the Bible Society, 30 per cent of Christian parents never read Bible stories to their children, and 61 per cent of children in Britain have never even heard the story of the Good Samaritan.[1]

However, there are signs of hope that the Holy Spirit is at work stirring people afresh to pray. New prayer movements like 24-7 are expanding rapidly. The 24-7 prayer movement began in 1999, but its inspiration goes back much further, to Count Von Zinzendorf in the eighteenth century and the Rule of Life adopted by the Moravian community:

• To be true to Christ (prayer)
• To be kind to others (justice)
• To take the gospel to the nation (mission)

Their commitment to setting up round-the-clock prayer stations has led the 24-7 prayer movement out into all sorts of practical initiatives, such as rescue shops in red-light districts, 'puke vans' taking drunken clubbers home, transitional housing for the home-less and drug addicts, and campaigns and prayer weekends against human trafficking. As Andy Freeman put it, 'It seems that when people commit to pray, God opens their eyes to the needs of the environment they live in and sends them out to make a difference . . . it's hard to simply pray and then do nothing at all.'[2]

A significant development in recent years has been the growth of religious communities that seek genuinely to be communities but are dispersed in nature, building on the tradition of the Franciscan Tertiaries. Some, such as the Northumbrian Community and the Community of St Chad in Lichfield Diocese, have developed through the revival of interest in Celtic spirituality; others, such as the Order of Mission based at St Thomas Philadelphia in Sheffield, have emerged through interest in fresh expressions of church and the 'new monasticism'. When a day was recently arranged at Lambeth Palace for leaders of religious communities, the organizers were overwhelmed by the numbers of prospective attenders, both from traditional and newer communities. When the new Community of St Anselm, based at Lambeth Palace, opened its website for applications, there were more than six applicants for every residential place.

Prayer and evangelism

But what is the relationship between prayer, spirituality and evangel-ism? If prayer is the wellspring of evangelism, why is it that in many dioceses or districts the evangelism group and the spirituality group have so little overlap? Does a deepening spiritual life neces-sarily lead outwards to more engagement in evangelism, or can an interest in spirituality sometimes become a substitute for those who have tried to do evangelism but found it difficult and uncom-fortable? Evangelism is always going to be an 'edgy' activity, in which we sometimes encounter rejection and opposition; it appeals to a more activist, rather than contemplative, personality type.

Yet evangelists and contemplatives need each other if the Church is to be effective in the process of making new disciples. Indeed, as Bishop Stephen Cottrell has said, 'Contemplatives make the best evangelists.' Unless rooted in prayer and contemplation, evangelism is always in danger of becoming a merely human endeavour, with success or failure being keenly felt by the evangelist as somehow their personal responsibility. And unless linked closely with the proclamation of the evangel, contemplative prayer can become inward-looking, focused on one's own relationship with God, to the exclusion of others.

The paradox is that evangelism is both God's work and ours. As St Augustine wrote, 'Pray as if it all depends on God, and work as if it all depends on you.' Or, as William Carey, founder of the Baptist Missionary Society, put it: 'Expect great things from God; Attempt great things for God!' And St Paul said, 'I planted, Apollos watered, but God gave the growth' (1 Corinthians 3.6). If that is so, intercession is as essential a part of the work of evangelism as proclamation. Interestingly, at Leading Your Church Into Growth conferences one of the examples given is that churches that begin to pray regularly in their intercessions for new members somehow seem to receive new members.

Contemplation is also essential for other reasons. As evangelists, if we don't intentionally spend time in the presence of God we are open to the danger of becoming like those celebrities who endorse products that we know they don't themselves use. Furthermore, it is only when we take time to know and listen to God that we are able to align our efforts and energies in accordance with his will. Sometimes our best efforts seem to yield little or no fruit, and we have all at times echoed Peter's heartfelt words in Luke 5.5, 'Master, we have worked all night long but caught nothing.' It is in times when we choose to be still, to wait and to seek Jesus' face afresh, that we are able to hear the whisper of his quiet instruction: 'Put out into deep water and let down your nets for a catch.'

The American theologian Stanley Hauerwas comments that the Church should always be engaged in doing things that make no sense if God does not exist.[3] Faced with a world in need, or even as a minister with a handful of competing churches (and church buildings) to care for, time spent in contemplation can seem like time wasted. But if God does exist, it is the most important thing we ever do. In Christian ministry, however much we try to do, the task is always unfinished, but if we spend more time in prayer, the small bits that we can do are more likely to be in tune with, or aligned with, what God is doing and therefore to be fruitful.

Spiritual or numerical growth?

In November 2010 Rowan Williams, then Archbishop of Canterbury, set out the first priority of the Church of England as being 'to take forward the spiritual and numerical growth of the Church'. This emphasis on spiritual as well as numerical growth is obviously important if the Church is to see the kind of 'good growth' that is the fruit of costly obedience to the gospel of Christ rather than the result of a desperate recruitment drive. Attendance figures can be given a short-term boost – by putting on enough pet services and Christingles – but that will not of itself produce committed disciples. Now that denominations are increasingly signed up to the priority of growth, we need to be careful about the kind of growth we are looking for and praying for – and especially the kind of growth we are measuring. As the business maxim puts it, we need to measure what we value, or we will end up valuing what we measure.

But what happens, say, when the aims of spiritual and numerical growth pull in opposite directions – which is more important? For example, in John chapter 6 Jesus is faced with a crowd of 5,000 who have just been fed and want to make him king by force, yet he challenges them with the selfishness of their motives (6.26); eventually the crowds drift away and Jesus is left with the 12. He asks them, 'Do you also wish to go away?' It is at this point, when in human terms his preaching might seem to have failed, that Peter makes his spiritual breakthrough, affirming, 'Lord, to whom can we go? You have the words of eternal life. We have come to believe and know that you are the Holy One of God' (6.67–69). Sometimes a congregation may need to go through a period of pruning, perhaps losing some members but taking the rest deeper in discipleship, before it can grow numerically again.

Desert or oasis?

A few years ago I spent a week trekking and camping in the Sinai desert. Reading the Bible in that austere landscape I realized afresh that, as David Runcorn put it, 'The Scriptures teach us that there is no path to God that does not pass through the wilderness. The God of the Bible is the God of the desert.'[4] I was leading daily Bible studies on the life of Moses, but I could have chosen any one of many figures whose faith was shaped in the desert – Abraham, Jacob, Elijah, John the Baptist, St Paul and, of course, Jesus. The time of greatest spiritual growth is not when all is going well and flourishing, but when everything is stripped away and we are left with God alone. There is something about the unforgiving landscape of the desert, where danger is never far away, that forces us to do serious business with God. In Scripture and in life, the school for discipleship is the desert rather than the oasis.

What kind of growth?

> You do not have to travel long in ways of prayer and spiritual life to discover that Christian growth is untidy, slow, inefficient, full of apparent detours, and frequently downright contradictory!
>
> (David Runcorn)[5]

Christians in the West have lived so long in the consumerist culture that we too easily equate evangelism with marketing, and God and Church as products to be 'sold' on the grounds of utility, how they meet our deepest human needs. On this mindset the size and growth of the Church is a sign of its success and worth. However, Eugene Peterson points out that the Church in America has been devastated by such consumerist assumptions:

> Our methods of going about our business are, by and large, counter to the gospel. Everyone thinks that if the church is doing it right they're going to have a lot of people. But the church, when it has been alive, has never been popular. Never.[6]

In Britain it is a particularly difficult calling to maintain a large and faithful congregation without falling into some of the consumerist values that imbue the culture.

The churches in Revelation that receive the most praise (Smyrna and Philadelphia) are not the outwardly successful ones like Laodicea ('I am rich, I have prospered, and I need nothing', 3.17), but those who know their affliction and poverty (2.9) and have but little power (3.8). A church that has spiritual depth and power may have none of the recognition, prestige or trappings of human success, but then the Church is God's instrument not to imitate the culture but to subvert it. Too often we equate the growth of the kingdom of God with the growth of the Church, and yet, as E. H. Peterson puts it in his chapter entitled 'The Subversive Pastor' (of his book *The Contemplative Pastor*), 'nowhere in Scripture or history do we see a church synonymous with the kingdom of God'.[7] Subversives are most effective when they are not recognized as posing any threat to the status quo. Perhaps the re-evangelization of our nation will happen not through the recreation of large 'Christendom' churches so much as through small subversive cells eating away at the foundations of our consumerist secularist ideology.

Evangelism as risk-taking

We live in a risk-averse culture, yet there is something fundamentally risky about evangelism, when we are called to proclaim afresh the Christian faith in each generation. We learn by trying out new ideas, and finding out what works and what doesn't, and so perhaps 'success' in evangelism should be measured not in how many come to us, our courses and events, but how far we have been willing to go to reach the lonely, the lost and the broken with the good news of God's grace. And maybe not by how easy we have made it to respond, but how hard; when the eager rich young ruler walked away sad, the disciples might have felt disappointed that Jesus had not made an easy win.

Time spent in prayer and contemplation should make us willing to take risks, in so far as it helps us to glimpse things from God's perspective. When we come down the mountain we see things differently. When Jesus has spent the whole night in prayer he then takes some pretty risky choices in his choice of 12 disciples – a Zealot and a tax collector working for the Romans, two whose nicknames are 'sons of thunder', and Judas Iscariot, to name but five. Was it a mistake to choose Judas as one of them, or was Jesus right to give him a chance and take a risk, willing in love to bear the personal cost if it all went wrong?

When Jesus learned from his father how to be a carpenter he doubtless made lots of mistakes, and plenty of bits of wood would have had to be discarded or (more likely) recycled for other things. So presumably in his ministry not everything that Jesus tried worked – we read in Capernaum that 'he could do no deed of power there' because of their lack of faith (Mark 6.5). When the blind man could only see 'men like trees walking', Jesus had another go. When the Syro-Phoenician woman answered him back, Jesus changed his mind and tried a different response. And asking those who had been healed not to tell anyone doesn't seem to have worked very well as a strategy (Mark 1.45; 7.36).

> Disturb us, Lord, when we are too pleased with ourselves,
> When our dreams have come true because we
>   dreamed too little,
> When we arrived safely because we sailed too close to
>   the shore . . .
> Disturb us, Lord, to dare more boldly,
> To venture on wilder seas where storms will show Your
>   mastery;
> Where losing sight of land, we shall find the stars.
> We ask you to push back the horizons of our hopes;
> And to push back the future in strength, courage, hope
>   and love.
> This we ask in the name of our Captain, who is Jesus
>   Christ.   (Sir Francis Drake)

Death and resurrection

It is not only in the desert and in trying new things that spiritual growth and formation happen, but also in suffering and persecution.

There is no greater reminder that making new disciples is God's work rather than ours than the spiritual power of suffering and martyrdom. Tertullian's great saying has become an axiom of church history: 'The blood of the martyrs is the seed of the church.' Visiting the ancient Coptic monasteries of Wadi Natrun in Egypt a few years ago, it was moving to learn how many times in history various monasteries had been attacked by raiders and all the monks martyred, only for new monks to appear and refound the community.

Prayer and evangelism

One of the striking features of *Common Worship* is the lack of any service on a theme of evangelism, or a liturgy to encourage prayer for evangelism or the work of making new disciples. This absence is found in the service books of other denominations too. Of course, the Book of Common Prayer is no better, written as it was in a Christendom context. However, now that our liturgy has been reshaped and updated in so many ways, its lack of engagement with the missionary context of today needs addressing.

Prayer walking is a custom that seems to have grown in recent years. Christians meet together for prayer and then spread out in pairs to walk around particular streets or areas, praying for each home and for the welfare of the local community, and then come back together to share and pray about what they have noticed or seen as they walked. This can be a particularly helpful practice when seeking God's guidance for how to reach out into a particular area. Prayer walking may be a way in which it is possible to harness the passion of pray-ers and evangelists together, to the mutual enrichment of both.

When I first went to Wellington, the doors of our imposing town centre church were locked for most of the week. I longed to see them open every day, but what stymied us was a fear of damage – apparently some youths had damaged the building when it was unattended 40 years before, and it had been locked ever since. However, when we had a tragedy in the town, with the murder of a local teenager, we opened the doors to allow young people to come in and pray and light a candle. Such was the appreciation from the local community that the church council plucked up the courage to agree to open the former day chapel permanently and to furnish it as a prayer room, complete with a comfortable sofa, prayer stations, quiet worship music, Bibles and Christian literature. Visitors regularly leave prayer requests in the box, which are prayed for at Morning Prayer the next day; we are frequently moved by the depth and intensity of these prayer requests, mostly from people who do not attend on a Sunday.

Forming disciples: teaching people to pray

If, as we argued in *EWWN*, Church can be defined as worship+ mission+community, or a 'worshipping missionary community', then teaching people to pray can itself be deeply evangelistic. The authors of the new Pilgrim course demonstrate this, beginning each session, right from the start of the first enquirers' unit, with a simple liturgy. Courses like Essence (discussed in Chapter 7) are aimed at people who see themselves as spiritual but not religious, and seek to introduce people to the Christian faith through exploring relaxation, contemplation and prayer. One of the strengths of Alpha is its powerful blend of community (the meal and small group), spiritual experience (the weekend away) and clear, relevant teaching.

Pilgrimage and gatherings at holy places have a long history of nurturing and encouraging discipleship. In the middle ages it was visits to view holy relics and pray at the shrines of saints. In our own day regular visits to festivals like Walsingham, to New Wine, to the Keswick Convention or to Greenbelt are significant in the growth of many Christians as disciples of Christ. Often people come back to their local church fired up with a deeper enthusiasm for worship, prayer and the Bible, though helping such people to readjust to the 'ordinariness' of their local church can sometimes be a challenge. Likewise, many of us have been formed in our youth by regular attendance at summer house parties and ventures, first as members and later as helpers then leaders.[8] The challenge for churches is how to help those who do not have the time or money to go on pilgrimage or attend camps or festivals to grow in prayer and discipleship at home.

Ian Adams is an Anglican priest who co-founded and became abbot of mayBe, an experimental religious community in Oxford. In his book *Cave Refectory Road*,[9] he takes three rhythms of monastic life – the solitary cave or cell, the refectory where monks share community and the road where monks go out in mission – and reimagines how we might build those three elements into our daily discipleship as Christians as we juggle the demands of home, work and family. One resource Adams offers is the Morning Bell,[10] a call to prayer that goes out each day by text, email and Twitter, in an attempt to offer and encounter space, and a way into a monastic rhythm of prayer.

In the context of a team ministry in east London, the Revd Jill Mowbray felt led to set up a house of prayer for her parish, in her own home.

My original vision was to deepen the prayer life of our parish and be a spiritual engine for a great many active ministries. It was also to deepen accountability in living more intentional Christian lives for a larger core of church members. It was to be a prayer resource for the overbusy in the city, seeking God's favour for the city, and be a place of contemplation and stillness to introduce this kind of prayer to folk who haven't experienced it.

We started a pattern of twice-weekly morning and evening prayer in the house (a brief 20 minutes, open to any), occasional community meals and some prayer events three times yearly, a 'special event' prayer day on a Saturday, an Advent day, a Lent day, and (in planning) an 'all-age' children and families day, to encourage people of all kinds in more focused times of prayer. We have a 'prayer-hut' in the garden, bookable by individuals for a 'quiet day' or a few hours. We hope this might be a resource to local

Christian leaders, as well as people in the parish who might not otherwise get to go on Retreat, because of lack of funds or lack of transport.

Now, we have a group of approximately 16 Companions, meeting weekly on a weeknight, in some ways resembling many of our existing LIFEGroups, but distinct in the following three ways. We are committed to developing a set of common shared values and a simple 'rule' or way of life. We are committed to resourcing together the wider ministry of the prayer house events. We are committed in an explicit way to a growing mutual accountability.

We believe that shared rhythms of prayer are the heartbeat for Christian community, and 'provocative Christianity' in Graham Tomlin's phrase. A deepening of our individual and corporate prayer lives should lead to stronger, clearer Christian witness, and more distinctive discipleship. We want to see God do more things in and through us in our locality and community, and we believe that deeper, more focused prayer is the root and source for this.

As we have seen, there are exciting signs of a renewal of prayer and the religious life in England today. As so often with the work of the Spirit, this movement of renewal is creating *new* patterns of prayer and community, rather than simply drawing more people into the old ones. As Jesus said, 'New wine must be put into fresh wineskins' (Luke 5.38).

6

Alpha revisited

Alpha is a safe space between the culture and the church
where questions of life can be explored.

(Al Gordon)

In 2005 we wrote that Alpha 'was the biggest single evangelistic
tool of the 1990s, and has helped many hundreds of thousands
of people in the UK and around the world to come to Christian
faith'. However, our research revealed significant concerns, even
among regular users of the course, about certain aspects of its
content and theology. In particular we recommended to Holy
Trinity Church Brompton (known as HTB, the home of Alpha),
and to those considering adopting the course, that they review the
theological balance of the talks – to include more on the Trinity,
the person of God the Father, the sacraments of the Church and
the pursuit of social justice, and shorter, more balanced sections
on the Holy Spirit and healing. Looking at the talks again ten years
later, there have been a host of minor changes and the anecdotes
have been updated, but the essential shape is unchanged.

Subsequent critiques

A number of substantial, critical evaluations of Alpha have appeared
since we conducted our research in Lichfield Diocese, notably
from a liberal Anglican perspective by Stephen Brian and from a
sociology of religion perspective by Stephen Hunt.[1] Brian concludes that Alpha does not really offer an opportunity to explore
the meaning of life (as its advertising claims) and that its teaching
is effective not so much in converting people to Christ as promoting the expansion of its own version of Christianity within the

existing Church. Hunt concludes that the vast majority of guests on Alpha are already in the Church or, at the very least, have something of a church background, and that Alpha's major achievement has been in extending charismatic Christianity to churches previously untouched by the Renewal Movement.

More illuminating, balanced and helpful is a PhD thesis by James Heard.[2] Heard writes as a 'critical insider', having been on the staff of HTB for five years, during which time he helped to lead many Alpha courses and was Alpha's publications editor. Heard acknowledges that his own theological position has moved towards a more middle of the road Anglican position since he left Alpha, but his inside knowledge of the Alpha International organization has enabled him to do very revealing qualitative research, based on six Alpha courses in different churches in which he took part as a helper.

Low-hanging fruit

Heard's study is fair but critical. He concludes that the sudden conversion stories, so prominent in *Alpha News*, are the exception rather than the rule. Of those attending the courses in his survey, 86 per cent were either already regular churchgoers or were from the 'open de-churched' category; that is, they had been baptized, had generally grown up with some church involvement, had left at some point and were open to the possibility of returning.[3] 'Significantly under-represented were the non-churched or and the closed de-churched. This raise the question of whether Alpha should start further back,' he says.[4] According to Richter and Francis's research in 1998, the 'open de-churched' accounted for only 20 per cent of the population, compared with 20 per cent who were 'closed de-churched' and 40 per cent who were completely unchurched. Steve Hollinghurst's research shows that these broad categories vary significantly with age, with the proportion of unchurched growing fast among the younger generations. This suggests that although Alpha is effective in evangelism, it predominantly draws from a fairly small – and shrinking – part of the population.

Our own anecdotal experience is that many churches are still using Alpha, and seeing people come to faith on the course, especially where churches are enthusiastic and willing to base church life around it, but there is increasing evidence that it is gradually getting harder to recruit guests onto the course.

Attracting and retaining guests

Despite considerable effort, four of the six courses Heard studied struggled to recruit guests, and around 30 per cent of guests dropped out during the course. One significant reason cited for people dropping out was the high number of leaders and helpers in each small group. The Alpha recipe recommends two leaders and two helpers in each small group, with eight guests. However, in some of the courses he studied there were more than four Christians in the group – for example, a Christian friend of a guest might come on the course as well; in all the courses there were fewer non-Christian guests than hoped for; and in several groups there were only two or three guests. Having recruited and trained plenty of leaders, churches were shy of telling some that they were not actually needed, leading to small groups where the guests could be heavily outnumbered by Christians, and feeling unable to discuss their questions and concerns freely.

In my experience of running enquirers' groups in my own parishes, I find it works best when the only Christians in the group are myself and one co-leader, and where the not-yet Christian guests feel able to help to shape the direction of the discussion. That means that it is more of a challenge for the leader but the guests are at ease and relaxed, which leads to a much more fruitful discussion than when the leaders feel relaxed but the guests are ill at ease and inhibited.

Besides getting the balance of Christians to non-Christians right, the other key issue for the effectiveness of small groups in Alpha is the quality of training given to the group leaders. The Alpha training manual encourages group leaders to let the guests answer their own questions. Yet in many local churches enthusiastic leaders and helpers try to jump in with the 'right answer', even before the guest has finished articulating a query, or before other guests have had a chance to comment on the question the guest has raised. This has the effect of stifling discussion, and was a major reason for guests dropping out of Alpha in the groups that Heard studied.

Another reason that selection and training of group leaders is so crucial on Alpha is that some of the most difficult and thorny issues are not covered in the talks at all, and are left for group leaders to deal with when raised in small groups – such as explaining the Trinity, creation versus evolution and what the Bible says about sex outside marriage and same-sex relationships.

Kerygma or catechesis

Heard asserts that a major area of tension on the course is Alpha's broad aim of trying to combine both mission and spiritual formation.[5] Alpha seeks to include both kerygma – the proclamation of the gospel to unbelievers – and catechesis – the instruction of new disciples in the Christian faith. This tension goes back to the origin of the Alpha course: this was originally designed as a discipleship tool for new Christians, but leaders quickly found that it was proving effective in reaching those who were not yet Christians.

However, the fact that Alpha fulfils a role in both mission and spiritual formation is not necessarily a weakness. The early Methodist class system is an example that was highly effective in combining both. As Martyn Atkins writes:

> The condition for admission into Methodist societies is also worth noting . . . Though they will have begun a journey of faith there's not even an assumption that a person seeking admission is already 'converted'. This broad, aspirational criterion for admission to a Methodist society is regarded by many as a jewel, highly attractive and deeply meaningful.[6]

Despite author Nicky Gumbel's vision for Alpha to be just the first term of a two-year process of initiation, very few churches offer any specific post-Alpha follow-up. Heard's findings tie in with our own research in *EWWN* in Lichfield Diocese, which found very little use of any of the Alpha follow-up courses. Significantly, this also seems to chime with HTB's own experience, where getting people to sign up for follow-on courses has proved difficult and the emphasis now is on keeping Alpha small groups together after the course and introducing them to one of the pastorates – that is, collections of three or four home groups. However, Heard quotes internal research from 2004 showing that only 4 per cent of those attending Alpha at HTB actually made the move into pastorates.[7] No figures are available from HTB about how many of those attending Alpha currently progress to join ongoing groups.[8]

Although Gumbel speaks of a 'two-year process of initiation', there is very little mention of baptism (only one paragraph) on either Alpha or the four follow-on courses written by him, and nothing on confirmation or the Eucharist. The reason given is that these are issues on which Christians disagree, but the result seems to be an unsacramental form of Christian initiation that lacks some of the essential ingredients of the catechumenate. Heard comments:

> For the majority of Catholics, Orthodox and Anglicans, it is inconceivable for a two-year programme of evangelism and discipleship not to stress the intrinsic link between baptism and evangelism, or to see baptism, confirmation (or equivalent) and the Eucharist as the goal of the initiation process.[9]

Heard's point would apply equally to Baptists, for whom, of course, baptism is an essential part of the process of making new disciples.

In view of Alpha's stated focus on 'stripping down the Gospel to its bare essentials' and concentrating on those things that all Christians agree on, it is striking that the Apostles' Creed does not make an appearance on Alpha. Of the four basic texts for Anglican initiation – the Lord's Prayer, the Apostles' Creed, the Summary of the Law and the Beatitudes[10] – the Lord's Prayer and the Summary of the Law are covered briefly on Alpha, the Beatitudes are in the follow-up course, Challenging Lifestyle, but the Creed is missed out altogether. By contrast, other areas on which Christians profoundly disagree – such as tongues, healing, 'power evangelism' – are covered extensively.

Alpha is changing

In *EWWN* we commented that 'after twelve years on the market with minimal revision it is beginning to look a bit dated in content and style'.[11] However, since the start of the Alpha Innovation programme in January 2013 there is no longer anything dated about the style and presentation of Alpha. A major rebranding exercise, led by the top 2012 Olympics branding agency Wolff Olins, changed everything in the attempt to reach their target demographic. Al Gordon, vice-president of Alpha International, explains:

> Alpha is aimed at a 24-year-old urban male Christian leader and his non-Christian friend. This is the hardest demographic to reach, and it is also the most digitally connected tribe – and it is the same tribe all over the world, in Canada or the US or Bombay or Africa. It is not that Alpha doesn't want to reach 78-year-old rural women, but the way to do so is to reach the 24-year-old urban male.[12]

To this end, the balding white man on the old logo has gone; there is no longer a person, just a question mark and the word 'Alpha'. It is no longer 'the Alpha course', it is just Alpha: 'Young people don't want to sign up for a course, it makes them think of tuition fees and a £20k debt.' Everything has been rebranded, and the styling of the website and promotional material is now *uber*-cool. A visit to Alpha's headquarters reveals floor upon floor of bright young creatives in front of Apple Macs. Including the staff of HTB and St Mellitus, there are around 300 paid employees, and Gumbel has more assistants dealing with his postbag than the Archbishop of Canterbury.

The appeal of the brand is clearly an important draw – on the website the first step on the 'Getting started' section is 'Design your logo'. The focus on brand has led to some complaints about the frequency of changes in the advertising material, leaflets and so on. This looks cool for those churches that can afford each year's latest design update, but for smaller and poorer churches it can be frustrating.

Alpha now starts slightly further back than it used to: what was the 'taster' Alpha supper talk is now week 1, and 'Who is Jesus?' doesn't appear until week 2. Considerable resource is being put into redoing and promoting the talks for younger audiences, and live web streaming from HTB, using younger speakers as well as Gumbel, is being used by many churches to good effect. The classic 15 talks by Gumbel are still available, though 'How does God guide us?' appears to be optional; two sets of DVDs are available, one of which leaves it out to compress the course to ten weeks. The introductory talk is no longer entitled 'Christianity: boring, untrue and irrelevant?' but rather 'Is there more to life than this?' And 'How can I be sure of my faith?' has become 'How can we have faith?'

All the talks are now available free from the website, and the scripts can be downloaded in Word format for editing at home, making running Alpha much cheaper and easier to customize. The website now offers Alpha in a variety of lengths and formats (see Table 6.1 overleaf).

The Alpha Youth film series, produced by two Canadians, Jason Ballard and Ben Woodman, has been a huge hit, leading to a massive increase in the number of Youth Alpha courses registered around the world. In fact the Canadian series has proved so popular that it is now being recommended by the Alpha website for adult groups in the UK, rather than the Gumbel videos. The fact that the presenters are Canadian gives it quite a cool and classless feel – we don't know whether the presenters are posh or poor. They have slimmed Alpha down to 12 talks: 'Who is the Spirit?' is combined with 'What does he do?', and 'What about the church?' with 'Telling others'. Such has been the positive reception to this series that Alpha are now filming a new British version of Alpha using the same format, with talks limited to 30 minutes, filmed creatively on location with no more than three minutes in any one place. Given the hefty cost of filming on location, the decision to make all these resources freely available online is a very generous gift to the wider Church from the members of Holy Trinity Brompton, which as a church substantially underwrites the costs of Alpha International.

Alpha for Students has its own 30-minute videos with Jamie Haith ('squeezed, squashed and spiced') – with the length slimmed

Table 6.1 The variety of Alpha courses

Alpha (45-minute talks by Nicky Gumbel filmed at HTB)	Alpha Youth (20-minute films with Ben and Jason shot in Canada and on location)	Alpha Students (30-minute talks by Jamie Haith filmed in front of a live audience)	Alpha Prisons (downloadable scripts but no films)
1 Is there more to life than this?	1 Life. Is this it?	1 Is this it?	1 Who is Jesus and why did he die?
2 Who is Jesus?	2 Jesus. Who is Jesus?	2 Who is Jesus?	2 Why do I pray?
3 Why did Jesus die?	3 Cross. Why did Jesus die?	3 Why did Jesus die?	3 Why and how should I read the Bible and how does God guide us?
4 How can we have faith?	4 Faith. How can I have faith?	4 How can I have faith?	4 The Holy Spirit. Who is he and what does he do? How can I be filled?
5 Why and how do I pray?	5 Prayer. Why and how do I pray?	5 Why and how do I pray?	5 Does God heal today and how can I resist evil?
6 Why and how should I read the Bible?	6 Word. Why and how do I read the Bible?	6 Why and how should I read the Bible?	6 How can we have faith and how can I make the most of the rest of my life?

7 How does God guide us?

(Weekend away)
8 Who is the Holy Spirit?

9 What does the Holy Spirit do?

10 How can I be filled with the Holy Spirit?

11 How can I make the most of the rest of my life?

12 How can I resist evil?

13 Why and how should I tell others?

14 Does God heal today?

15 What about the church?

7 Follow. How does God guide us?

8 Spirit. Who is the Holy Spirit and what does he do?

9 Fill. How can I be filled with the Holy Spirit?

10 Evil. How can I resist evil?

11 Healing. Does God heal today

12 Church. What about the church and telling others?

7 Who is the Holy Spirit and what does he do?

8 How can I be filled with the Holy Spirit?

9 How does God guide me to make the most of my life?

10 What about evil and does God heal today?

11 What about the church and telling others?

down from 15 to 11 talks. As well as the same combinations of talks as in Alpha Youth above, 'What about evil?' is combined with 'Does God heal today?', and the talk on guidance with 'How can I make the most of the rest of my life?' Alpha for Prisons cuts down the whole course to six sessions. As Al Gordon comments, 'You can make Alpha shorter – we run it shorter to fit university terms and remand prisons – but what you lose is time for relationships to grow.'[13]

Contextualization

Around the time of our first book, Alpha was being critiqued by Pete Ward, Martyn Percy and others for contributing to a process of McDonaldization.[14] Ward argued that by reducing evangelism to a recipe to be followed (and not deviated from), Alpha was hindering the necessary local contextualization that must take place if the gospel is to be heard authentically in the culture of its hearers. Reflecting on Alpha 12 years on, it is fascinating to see how extensively Alpha is being customized and adapted to make it more effective in particular contexts, such as with students, young people, prisons, the elderly and so forth. What is striking also is how the whole brand and style of Alpha is being completely reworked (as we noted earlier) to contextualize it as an evangelistic tool to reach each target context – for example, the digital world of the 24-year-old urban male.

Alpha still has its famous copyright statement – but the number of specialist courses (students, prisons, seniors, youth, forces etc.) and the variety of speakers and video resources contribute to a rather more relaxed regime. As stated above, all the talks and scripts can now be freely downloaded for local adaptation – although each script is carefully colour coded to show where you can substitute a different anecdote, and which text should not be changed without emailing for permission.

Alpha and sexuality

The latest edition of *Searching Issues* – the Alpha manual designed to equip small group leaders to answer the questions most commonly asked by guests – still has seven chapters, but the ones on 'sex before marriage' and 'homosexuality' have now disappeared. They have been replaced with 'Does religion do more harm than good?' and 'Is faith irrational?' The promotional material says that 'tough questions require straight answers', but have they ducked out of giving straight answers on these two hot potatoes?

We took up the surprising absence of sexual issues with Al Gordon, asking whether it was true that interest in sex had declined markedly since the rise of Alpha. Gordon admitted that the decision wasn't taken because young people were no longer asking questions about sex, but rather:

> When you come on Alpha I hope that three things happen: you are welcomed and you don't feel judged or condemned (people expect the church to be full of homophobes), you meet Jesus, you have an experience of the Holy Spirit and your whole operating system gets changed – that's when issues of discipleship come up.

Alpha's position on sexuality can be defended on the grounds of research, which shows that people tend to come to Christian faith through a process of three stages, summarized as belonging, believing, behaving. Rather than becoming a Christian and then looking for a church to join, the evidence is that people tend to begin attending church or a small group first, and according to the welcome and acceptance they encounter gradually come to faith and commitment; they then sort out issues of behaviour after that. In seeking to model acceptance rather than judgement, Alpha can claim to be following the example of Jesus, as discussed in Chapter 4.

However, Alpha's approach may be open to the criticism that it is being timid or pragmatic, recognizing that society is changing and stepping back from challenging people on one of the most critical areas where the expectations and behaviour of young people are in such contrast to the traditional teaching of the Church. If so, Alpha could be seen as taking a different approach from that of Jesus, who tended to raise the bar and challenge people to discipleship not in the non-controversial areas of their lives, but at the place where his claims most demanded change.

To the rich young ruler he talked about money, telling him to go and sell all that he had, and in his encounter with the woman at the well he brought up her sex life, telling her to go and get her husband.

The Alpha talk on 'How can I make the most of the rest of my life?' still affirms marriage as the God-given context for sexual relations, and includes this comment: 'And I've never met anybody who's said to me, "I really regretted that I waited until my wedding day." I've met lots of people who said, "I really wish I had waited, because I've made a mess of my life."'[15] Whether same-sex sexual relationships are acceptable for Christians is not discussed at all in the current Alpha resources. So we pressed Gordon about how and when issues of sex outside of marriage and same-sex relationships were dealt with in the discipleship process at Holy Trinity Brompton, the home of Alpha. For example, if you had enjoyed Alpha and begun to attend church and volunteer for things, when would you be challenged or told that you couldn't take on certain roles (for example, a home group leader) if you were co-habiting or in a same-sex relationship? Gordon replied, 'I have absolutely no idea. I am sorry.'

When we quizzed Mark Elsdon-Dew, Communications Director at Holy Trinity Brompton, about HTB's teaching on sexuality, he answered:

> Those two chapters [that have been dropped from *Searching Issues*] reflect what Nicky Gumbel felt when he wrote them 25 years ago. However, people feel slightly differently about this issue today than we did ten years ago – I know Nicky does. As with the rest of the Church of England, discussions are ongoing at HTB, as we try to sensitively discern what the Holy Spirit is saying.[16]

What about the future of Alpha?

When we asked Gordon about his vision for the future of Alpha, he explained that his vision for 30 years' time was that Alpha would 'have changed from a movement to an idea', an idea that had become embedded in the life of the whole Church; and that discussion of Alpha would have moved from personality to concept. 'I am not interested in keeping a ministry going – that is dispiriting . . . Nicky and I don't give a fig about Alpha – if we found another course that was more effective at introducing people to Jesus we'd ditch Alpha tomorrow.'

On the other hand, it is striking that although since Alpha innovation the appearance and feel of the course have changed completely, the shape of the syllabus remains very much the same. When we met Tim May, then head of Alpha UK, we asked him whether he was considering any major reworking of the talks. He said, 'Theology is a question for Nicky – totally.' When we asked another Alpha insider whether there was likely to be any significant revision to the content of the Alpha course in the future the reply was, 'Not as long as Nicky is around. You would have more chance of changing canon law.' Another commented, 'He is very reluctant to change a winning formula, something that God has chosen to bless so mightily.'

There will be those reading this chapter who have personal cause to give thanks to God for Alpha. Alpha may not be perfect, but it is still, 25 years on, being used by God to bring huge numbers of people to faith in Christ, and has provided a model of process evangelism that many others have been able to follow and adapt.

Christ Church W4 has been running Alpha for ten years but recently ran Alpha two terms in a row for the first time. They were surprised and delighted to find it filled up and met a need, including attracting three people totally unconnected to church who came through the central Alpha website having seen the branded banners on the side of the church for many years. Richard Moy, vicar of Christ Church, comments:

The Holy Spirit day was particularly moving for the most sceptical of these, who found that she encountered God at several times during the day despite her outwardly cynical protests. Alpha works! Just today I encountered someone who came to faith in Christ on Alpha from another world religion background. She was serving on the HTB leadership conference team! Another young man has recently applied to be on our staff team. He wrote to me to say: 'Jesus found me in the most amazing way!! Me and my sister grew up in a Sikh household, till a pastor came to our house, who was going from door to door telling people about Jesus. He played us an Alpha video and invited us to his church around the corner. My atheist farther gave his heart to Christ two weeks later, followed by me ended up giving her heart to Christ.' The key to Alpha working in churches is having some people with a heart, passion and prayer life for evangelism. It's not a substitute for that, but linked together it makes a potent force. We're going to stick with it.

7

Courses: shorter spans, longer bridges?

---•◦•---

> People need ever longer to get their heads around the
> faith and will commit ever shorter amounts of time.
>
> (Bob Jackson)

In this chapter we examine what alternatives there are to Alpha,
how the world of evangelistic courses is changing, including how
other well-known brands are adapting, what tools are now available
at the first contact or 'pre-Alpha' stage, and what ongoing discipleship courses and resources are available for the 'post-Alpha' stage.

When we wrote *EWWN* the Alpha course had recently exploded
onto the scene, blazing a trail for an evangelism strategy based
on process rather than event. The principles of Alpha – 15 sessions,
eating together, small-group discussions – were beginning to be
copied in a variety of other process evangelism courses, including
Emmaus and Christianity Explored.

In 1999, 61 per cent of parishes in Lichfield Diocese had begun
to offer some sort of process evangelism course on a regular basis;
over 6,000 lay people had attended these courses, and of these,
22 per cent had come to Christian faith during the course. The
research showed that the three most popular courses scored almost
identical percentages of people coming to faith, indicating that it
was the concept, rather than a particular brand, that was the key
to fruitfulness. What was most surprising was that the category of
'other courses', which included a variety of lesser-known courses
and parishes' own home-made courses, scored a significantly higher
percentage of people coming to faith (27 per cent) than the published brands, despite the fact that when asked, clergy were much
more inclined to recommend the well-known brands than their
own home-made courses.

We identified a number of reasons why home-grown or locally adapted courses were proving the most fruitful. The spirituality of the locally produced course will fit that context, making it easier for a person to transfer from attending the course to Sunday worship; the local course leaders know their course members, and so can adapt the material to start where their members are and choose what they are most likely to engage with; and, very practically, the more you put into preparing a course the more you get out of it – whereas it can be a bit too easy for a hard-pressed leader simply to take the DVD off the shelf and copy the questions out of the manual.

Are courses still the answer?

Since we wrote our first book, the landscape of courses has changed hugely. Some courses have disappeared, new ones have been written, and generally courses are becoming shorter, both in the length of the talks and the number of sessions. The key dilemma facing those who produce courses, and churches that want to use them, as we have noted, is that people need ever longer to get their heads around the faith and will commit ever shorter amounts of time. They are starting much further back along the road, with little or no residual knowledge of the faith, and yet lead the kind of busy and complicated lives where it is increasingly less possible to sign up for a 15-week course.

Six or seven weeks seems a more manageable commitment to ask enquirers to make, but that means that churches need to diversify and offer more courses of shorter duration rather than expecting that one 15-session course can do it all. The title for this chapter is inspired by wide estuaries like the River Forth in Scotland, which was too wide for a single-span bridge but was successfully spanned in the nineteenth century by the Forth rail bridge, consisting of a series of shorter spans resting on intermediate piers. Rather than expecting those with the first glimmerings of interest in the Christian faith to commit themselves to a single course of 15 or more sessions, it is more realistic and effective to invite them to take part in a shorter initial course and then encourage them to sign up for a variety of subsequent short courses according to their need. It is significant that the Church of England's new Pilgrim course is appearing as a series of shorter, six-week courses, which can be offered as 'standalone' or part of a sequence.

The second dilemma is that people seem much less keen to sign up for a course at all than in previous decades, unless they are personally invited to do so, as we noted in Chapter 2. Thus, in order to be effective, courses need to be part of a whole-church disciple-making culture, where church members make the first contact with non-Christians on their own front line, can invest time one to one and invite people to join a course once they have crossed the initial thresholds – from distrust to trust and from being uninterested to being curious about the person of Jesus. And since courses are shorter and less comprehensive than they used to be, the ministry of the friend or accompanier will be equally important after the first course is completed, as the enquirer considers what to do next.

What are the alternatives to Alpha?

Christianity Explored/Discipleship Explored

This course is written and presented by Rico Tice, from All Souls, Langham Place. The third edition of Christianity Explored (2011) reduces the length of the course from ten weeks to seven, with one day rather than a weekend away. Overall the course now has ten talks rather than 15, with the sessions on discipleship issues – church family, Holy Spirit, prayer, the Bible, the devil and assurance – omitted. This makes for a manageable length in today's culture, but makes it all the more important to encourage those who complete Christianity Explored to go on to study the eight-session follow-up, Discipleship Explored. However, as one can see from Table 7.1 overleaf, there is no longer a single session on the Holy Spirit, even if one completes both courses. According to Rico Tice, 'Christianity is about Christ', but the lack of emphasis on the Holy Spirit (compared to Alpha) and on God the Father or the Trinity (compared to Pilgrim) will raise issues for some Christians considering using the material.

Table 7.1 Topics covered in Christianity Explored and Discipleship Explored

Christianity Explored (2001)	Christianity Explored (2011 edition)	Discipleship Explored (2012)
1 Introduction	1 Good News. What are we doing here?	1 Confident in Christ
2 Jesus – who is he?	2 Identity. Who is Jesus?	2 Living in Christ
3 Jesus – why did he come?	3 Sin. Why did Jesus come?	3 Standing together in Christ
4 Jesus – his crucifixion	4 The Cross. Why did Jesus die?	4 Transformed by Christ
5 Jesus – his gift of grace	5 Resurrection. Why did Jesus rise?	5 Righteous in Christ
6 Jesus – his resurrection	6 Grace. How can God accept us?	6 Knowing Christ
		7 Rejoicing in Christ
	Day away	8 Content in Christ
	The Sower. Listen carefully	
Weekend away	James and John. Ask humbly	
7 You're never alone – the church family	Herod. Choose wisely	
8 You're never alone – the Holy Spirit		
9 You're never alone – prayer	7 Come and die. What does it	
10 You're never alone – the Bible	mean to follow Jesus?	
11 The motivation to keep going		
12 What is a Christian?		
13 The devil and assurance		
14 Choices – King Herod		
15 Choices – James and John		

The new edition of Christianity Explored has less sin, less rugby and more grace than the original, making the approach slightly less hearty and more inclusive – though still with the original strapline, 'You are more sinful than you ever imagined but more loved than you ever dreamed.' Both courses combine very high-quality video, shot on location, with a strong emphasis on getting participants to read the Bible right from the first day of the course. Christianity Explored is based on Mark's Gospel, and Discipleship Explored on Philippians. The emphasis on forming a personal habit of regular Bible reading reflects the course's evangelical provenance, but is particularly helpful in a busy culture where even the keenest participants are not able to make every week of a course, because of work or family commitments. The leader's handbooks are very comprehensive, including full talk scripts, but are difficult to use in conjunction with the members' handbooks: the page numbers and layout are different, so it is not clear what the members have in front of them without looking over their shoulders!

Pilgrim

Commissioned by the Archbishops' Council of the Church of England, this course was published in 2013. One great advantage is that it offers a series of bite-sized chunks – six weeks at a time being good for those who find a longer course too much of a commitment. The short video clips and audio are all available to download free from the website, meaning that you only need to buy the participants' handbooks. It is very easy to run and requires little preparation by the leader – it doesn't take long to glance at the video clip and read through the two short essays. However, the excellently produced handbooks are confusing in one respect – they give no indication as to when to show the video clip: indeed, we know of leaders who have used Pilgrim without realizing that there were video clips to introduce each session.

Pilgrim builds on the catechumenate model developed by Emmaus (see below), including the reception of key texts, such as the Beatitudes, the Creeds, the Lord's Prayer and the Commandments, with appropriate liturgical markers to celebrate stages on the journey. The use of liturgical texts and the way a brief liturgy is

Table 7.2 Pilgrim – a course for the Christian journey, comprising eight six-week modules

	What do Christians believe?	How do Christians know and worship God?	How do Christians behave?	What is the Christian vision for the world?
Follow stage: Do you turn to Christ?	1 Turning to Christ	2 The Lord's Prayer	3 The Commandments	4 The Beatitudes
Grow stage: Will you continue in the Apostles' teaching and fellowship?	1 The Creeds	2 The Eucharist	3 The Bible	4 Church and kingdom

included at the start of every session fulfils the twin aim of forming people as disciples through prayer, and also making a good transition between what is experienced in the group and what is offered in the local church on a Sunday. Pilgrim has a broad appeal theologically, including writers from different traditions. The fact that the first unit is based on the six questions from the baptism service makes it a good resource to use for enquirers thinking about being baptized, although it assumes a fair amount of background and education (see Table 7.2).

The style of Pilgrim will not appeal to everyone. The initial 'Turning to Christ' unit seems to be quite churchy for those making perhaps a first contact with church. However, while the 'churchiness' of Pilgrim may be awkward for enquirers unfamiliar with the culture, it may actually help them in making the transition into church, in that there is less of a contrast between the experience of the course and the experience of Sunday worship. It also feels a bit highbrow – the main teaching content is delivered by means of recordings of bishops reading out essays, and the first session makes reference to Athanasius, Ambrose, Anselm and Bonhoeffer, without any explanation as to who these persons were.

Setting as homework short readings from the Fathers and other Christian writers is given priority over encouraging people to develop a habit of regular Bible reading. In 'Turning to Christ' it is not until the end of session 3 that there is the first tentative suggestion for personal Bible reading at home: 'Perhaps read through the story of Jesus' death and resurrection in one of the Gospels.' However, no suggestion is given as to which Gospel to turn to or which chapter to begin reading. Our experience of using Pilgrim in fairly well-read middle-class parishes is that when participants were asked to comment on the readings from the past week many had not in fact read them, and those who had didn't seem to have connected with them.

There is a strong reliance in Pilgrim on *lectio divina* as almost the only way of reading and understanding Scripture, rather than perhaps offering it as one approach among many. Participants are asked to read the Bible passage in the booklet several times, aided by only minimal explanatory notes, and to pick out a word or phrase that strikes them and comment on it. Reading the passage from the booklet rather than from the Bible itself may make it easier, but means that the biblical context is neither apparent nor easy to check. *Lectio divina* is certainly in fashion in the Church of England at present, and encourages people to ask not 'What does the passage mean?' but rather, 'What does it say to me?' However, when using it with groups of enquirers who have no prior Bible knowledge there is a danger that the sharing could become a pooling of ignorance that misses the essential meaning of the passage.

Emmaus

Unlike Pilgrim (one friend of ours commented, 'Almost every piece of post I open includes a flyer for Pilgrim'), very little effort was ever put into promoting the Emmaus course (first published 1996), despite the huge amount of work that went into creating the 15-session Nurture course, a number of comprehensive Growth modules and the Youth Emmaus course. All the Emmaus resources are still available to order but they are no longer being promoted, and various modules were being remaindered in the last Church House Publishing January sales. Talking to the head of CHP, the

Table 7.3 Content of the Emmaus Growth modules

Knowing God	Living the gospel
	Knowing the Father
	Knowing Jesus
	Come, Holy Spirit
Growing as a Christian	Growing in prayer
	Growing in the Scriptures
	Being Church
	Growing in worship –
	understanding the sacraments
	Life, death and Christian hope
Christian lifestyle	Living images
	Overcoming evil
	Personal identity
	Called into life
Your kingdom come	The Beatitudes
	The kingdom

strategy seems to be to let Emmaus wither on the vine, simply printing on demand as needed.

This is a huge pity, as the Growth modules provide a great variety of short courses that can be used and adapted according to need as follow-on materials for those who have completed Alpha, Discipleship Explored or Pilgrim. Perhaps a better way to secure the ongoing availability of these resources might be (if the authors were agreeable) to take a leaf out of Alpha's book and make all the units available digitally online, so that people could browse them and download them for free.

The four Emmaus Growth books comprise 15 short courses with photocopiable handouts (see Table 7.3).

Believe

This is a very watchable DVD-based course of excellent quality produced in 2008 by Catholic Faith Exploration (CaFE). It is based on the Nicene Creed and is presented by David Payne – Director of CaFE – and attractively shot on a variety of relevant locations including the Holy Land, Nicaea, Rome, Oxford, Cambridge and London. Sessions last approximately 35 minutes and feature interviews with well-known Christians such as Jackie Pullinger, Henri Nouwen, Delia Smith and Lord Alton.

While coming from a Roman Catholic stable and designed for use with the Rite of Christian Initiation of Adults (RCIA), we have used it very effectively in an Evangelical Anglican parish setting as a whole-church Lent course. We left out the most 'Catholic' session (5, on the Holy Spirit and the Church) to fit into the five weeks leading up to Holy Week, and needed to give the occasional rider or explanation before some of the programmes (to explain certain words like magisterium!), but group members loved it, and found it stimulating and helpful. We are not aware of any other resource on the Creed of remotely as good quality from an Anglican stable, and could imagine it working well as an adult confirmation or post-confirmation course, particularly in a middle- or high-Anglican parish. The sessions are:

- Session 1: Why we believe
- Session 2: How we believe
- Session 3: Almighty Father
- Session 4: Jesus Christ
- Session 5: Holy Spirit and Church
- Session 6: Coming Kingdom

There is a very short leader's guide, posters and a members' booklet. It is available from Catholic Faith Exploration, <http://faithcafe.org/collections/believe-reflections-on-the-creed>. Each pack includes two DVDs, a music CD, a sample booklet, promotional material, plus a *Knowing the Father's Love* DVD. It is not cheap (£79.95), so it may be worth asking around to see if another local church or your local denominational office already has a copy you could borrow.

Compass/Disciple

Compass (2013) and Disciple (2004) are two high-quality courses from the Methodist Church. Full details can be found at <www.methodist.org.uk/deepening-discipleship/small-groups/key-resources>. Compass is a short eight-session course that introduces the Christian faith to those who wish to explore its meaning. Like any compass, it relates to a particular map and the one intended is Christian discipleship in the Methodist Church. The sessions are as follows:

- Session 1: Glimpses of God (the Creator)
- Session 2: Meeting Jesus today
- Session 3: The difference Jesus makes (the Cross)
- Session 4: Empowered by the Holy Spirit
- Session 5: Life together (the Church)
- Session 6: Engaging with Scripture
- Session 7: Following Jesus (decision to follow)
- Session 8: Called by name (initiation – baptism or confirmation)

Participants need to purchase their own booklets (£5 each), but leader's notes for each session can be downloaded free from the website.

One of the strengths of Compass – like the Roman Catholic Believe course – is that it is confident and clear about the denomination it comes from and in which it seeks to nurture enquirers and new believers. Each session of Compass has a particular section on 'the Methodist emphasis' – what the Methodist tradition has to bring to the particular topic. This is something that tends to be missing from many of the courses arising from an Evangelical Anglican milieu, which are often consciously seeking to be useful beyond their own denomination, and as a result are less clear and effective in helping enquirers to understand and value the particular tradition of their local church.

The second course, Disciple, is a year-long, 34-session Bible study course designed to help people read most of the Bible (70 per cent in total) in a year and be transformed by it. It originated from the Methodist Church in the USA but has been used in British Methodist churches for the last 15 years. It is stretching – participants need to set aside half an hour a day for their own intensive reading of Scripture, as well as two hours for a weekly meeting. The accompanying DVD offers input from biblical scholars to introduce each section, and PowerPoint materials are available too. However, it does not aim at head knowledge, but at transformation – to transform rather than inform. Its strapline is 'Becoming Disciples through Bible study', and many participants have gone on to train for leadership roles in the Church afterwards.

What is available for the pre-Alpha stage?

Start!/Moving On!

Published by CPAS in 2003, this short six-session course, with a consciously working-class, non-book culture edge to it, has proved popular in many churches wanting a pre-Alpha or pre-catechumenate resource. However, the films have dated very quickly – for example, they visit a video shop, and one of the interviewees talks about the attack on the Twin Towers on 9/11.

Following a decision by CPAS to discontinue Start!, the course has now been taken over by Leading Your Church Into Growth (LYCIG), and a brand new version is due to be released by Easter 2016. This version is not just an update, but incorporates a slightly broader and more nuanced explanation of sin (not only what we do, but also what others do to distort God's image in us) and the atonement. In the new films Robin Gamble, the author and well-known evangelist, is joined by three young presenters, and various locations include Blackpool and the south-east of England.

The Moving On! course, designed as a follow-up to Start!, has worked very well in many parishes. Moving On! provides seven interactive, small-group sessions. Each is based around a lively 15-minute DVD programme that includes location-based input and a thought-provoking personal story, and has photocopiable handouts. Beginning with course members' current experience, Moving On! is designed to help them:

- consider the benefits and challenges of being a follower of Jesus;
- be active and committed members of the Church;
- explore Christian worship;
- grow in their relationship with God;
- explore the Trinity and the Holy Spirit;
- think about Christian stewardship;
- be wholehearted disciples.

Uncover

Produced by the Universities and Colleges Christian Fellowship (UCCF) in 2011, Uncover is a great resource to equip people to read Luke's Gospel with a friend (<www.uccf.org.uk/uncover>). Creatively produced, a 'cool' pocket-sized Gospel is accompanied by a set of background notes and questions for discussion. The pitch is to encourage people to uncover, investigate and examine the evidence by reading the original source document for themselves. As the author, Becky Manley Pippert, says in the introduction:

> When I was an agnostic I investigated various religions, until one day it occurred to me that I had never read the Bible. I realised that for the sake of intellectual integrity I couldn't reject something I had never examined . . . Whatever your story, one thing is certain: it's impossible to make an informed decision without first investigating the evidence.

Rico Tice, the originator of Christianity Explored, commends the Uncover material as having made a significant difference to the fruitfulness of university missions he has led recently – many non-Christians attended the meetings because Christian students were already reading the Bible with a non-Christian friend, and so they had someone they could easily invite to hear a Christian speaker. Designed for untrained 18-year-old students, with simple questions to discuss, backed up with online resources that can be accessed by QR codes from a smartphone, this beautifully produced tool is having a big evangelistic impact within colleges and universities in Britain.

However, it can equally well be used by ordinary church members in local churches. The great strength is that church members don't need training. Everything is provided; they simply need to commit to meeting with an interested friend once a week for seven weeks, and by so doing they share not only the gospel but also their very selves (1 Thessalonians 2.8). A second Uncover course, based on John's Gospel, is now available.

Table Talk/Puzzling Questions

Founded by Paul Griffiths in 1997, the Ugly Duckling Company (<www.uglyducklingcompany.com>) produces high-quality resources to stimulate conversations, attempting to create spaces for people to explore the big and not-so-big questions of life. They are designed to be relevant for the first contact/pre-Alpha stage. The first step might be to invite people to a men's breakfast based around Table Talk, then invite those interested to join a six-session Puzzling Questions course, then maybe go on to one of the well-known courses.

Table Talk is a conversational card game. It creates space to 'explore' the questions of life, 'articulate' your thoughts and 'engage' with the opinions of others. A variety of Table Talk packs are available. In addition, there are a series of apps on the Apple App Store and Google Play Store. Every box contains six big themes. For each of the themes there is an introduction card and 16 specific questions. The idea is that six to eight people gather at a table, a theme is chosen, the introduction card is read, and the 16 question cards are placed on the table. One card is picked and the question posed to the group; when someone else is ready to ask a question, a different card is picked up. Games last on average 20–40 minutes, and could follow on well from a drink or some food beforehand.

Beth Cope, a pioneer minister, writes:

> We took Table Talk for Easter out into a café, gathering four to six people to share, laugh – and sometimes cry – while discussing things that matter but we somehow don't often talk about. Each week, we'd get out a pack of 16 starter questions, spread them out, and take it in turns to explore topics like 'Can tomorrow be better than today?' or 'Why do bad things happen to good people?'
>
> We've noticed people at tables around us listening, perhaps starting to ponder the questions themselves. Maybe one day they'll join in! Some questions are light-hearted: 'What would you be prepared to do for charity?' Some are practical: 'Want are your top tips for coping with a difficult situation?' Others start to go deeper: 'Where in your life do you encounter evil?' Reading from professionally

produced cards somehow makes it easier to ask things we'd otherwise not dare.

We've kept it informal: a few core people and most just coming once or twice. Personal invitations have made all the difference. People want to keep coming, so we're going to try out some of the other box sets. The tablet app works nicely at home – but using the cards seems more accessible in a public space.

Puzzling Questions is a video-based six-week course exploring some of life's deeper questions. The course looks at some of the most popular questions asked by those who aren't Christians but are interested in spirituality. The questions explored are as follows:

- Who am I?
- What is God like?
- What happens after I die?
- How can I be happy?
- Why is there suffering in the world?
- What is the spiritual realm and how does it impact my life?

The idea is that as people journey through the course with others interested in reflecting on life's big questions, they are given the opportunity to consider what they think and talk it through with others.

Essence

Written by Rob Frost and published by Share Jesus International in 2002, Essence is a six-week course designed to be attractive and accessible to those who would see themselves as on a spiritual journey, but might not have considered the Christian tradition as having much to offer those who are interested in body, mind and spirit. It is badged as a course designed 'to stimulate a deeper spiritual life, drawing from the teachings of Jesus and the Christian mystics'. The style is laid-back and unthreatening, and very experiential – relaxation exercises, making bracelets, smashing pots, modelling in dough. Essence is designed to take place in a non-religious building, and could be run as an evening class in a local college. The Bible is used as a resource in each of the sessions, all of which end with a prayer in the name of Jesus. The sessions consist of six 'journeys':

- Journey 1: so far – bonding, belonging, community, touch, spiritual highs and lows
- Journey 2: within – identity, image, perception, affirmation
- Journey 3: to a better world – a perfect creation, the eco-system, destruction, creator, stewardship, partnership
- Journey 4: to wholeness – body, mind, spirit, emotions, physical and mental pain
- Journey 5: to spirituality – spirituality, religious experience, seeking God, types of prayer, coming into God's presence
- Journey 6: to the future – hopes and dreams, the future, eternity

The whole course is available for free download from <www.sharejesusinternational.com/resources-home>.

Some other courses worth looking at

- **Christianity Explained (Michael Bennett, 2006)**
  This six-session evangelism course, based on Mark's Gospel, from the Good Book Company, assumes that people will know little or nothing of the Christian faith. The A4 manual costs £9.99 and includes photocopiable pages for group members. Details from <www.thegoodbook.co.uk/training/outreach-training/christianity-explained>.
- **Knowing God Better (David Payne, 2011)**
  Available from Catholic Evangelisation Services, this seven-session relaxed and practical course includes mime, music, testimonies and opportunities for prayerful reflection. The DVD with leader's pack costs £24.99. The pack includes Scripture reflection hand-outs for participants, which can be photocopied. Details from <www.faithcafe.org>.
- **Now a Christian (Peter Graystone, undated)**
  This free email-based course from Church Army is designed to help you discover the difference that having a relationship with Jesus can make to your life. It involves a daily email for

five weeks, with a link to an interactive website on the fourth day of each week. Details from <www.nowachristian.org>.

- **Simply Christianity (John Dickson, 1999)**
  Based on the Gospel of Luke, the goal of this five-part course is to surprise and challenge ordinary non-Christian people (whether churched or unchurched) with the unique story of Jesus Christ as told by Luke. Student manuals cost £2.80 each, with discounts available for bulk purchases, and leader's manuals £8. Details from <www.thegoodbook.co.uk/simply-christianity-student-manual>.

A useful resource

- More information about these and other courses can be found on the **Disciplekit** website, a new online resource from the Church Pastoral Aid Society that offers extensive reviews of small-group resources for adults and children who are enquiring about Christianity, beginning the Christian journey or growing along the way (<www.disciplekit.org>).

8

Fresh expressions: the way to the future?

———◦•◦———

The changing nature of our missionary context requires
a new inculturation of the gospel within our society.
                                                (Graham Cray)

Fresh expressions: a remarkable success story

As we explored in Chapter 1, church growth is a challenge in contemporary Britain. The bald statistical reality is of steadily declining
attendance at Sunday worship. But while that simple fact is widely
attested and now also accepted, even by those who might have
wished to interpret the figures differently, a look behind the headline attendance figures reveals more. The expansion of what have
become known as 'fresh expressions of church' runs completely
counter to the general trend, and as such is a source of a great
deal of good news, but also may conceal other and potentially
more serious challenges.

The inspiration behind fresh expressions of church is summed
up well by Mike Moynagh:

> Church no longer has the option, if ever it had, of relating
> to people as if they were all the same. It has to engage with
> them appropriately, a task that has been described as con-
> textualization. Contextualizing the church is an attempt
> to be church in ways that are both faithful to Jesus and
> appropriate to the people the church serves. It assumes that
> the shape of church can change according to the situation.
> Churches will look different because they are engaging with
> different people.[1]

CONTEXT
SHAPE OF CHURCH PEOPLE

We explored the concept of fresh expressions of church in *EWWN*[2] when it was still new to the life of the Church in England. Since then the literature recording a huge range of new ventures is extensive, and hard evidence of the major impact fresh expressions are now having in the life of the Church has been gathered by the Church Army's Research Unit. Their research into attendance at fresh expressions of church, being undertaken across a growing number of Church of England dioceses, is coming up with a fairly consistent pattern of 10 per cent of members of the Church of England now worshipping in the context of fresh expressions. This is an enormously exciting figure.

Planting new churches in not new, of course. Britain's cities pay tribute to the scale of Victorian church building with spacious parish churches standing close to imposing Nonconformist chapels. Later, daughter churches and mission halls were set up in the early twentieth century as new housing expanded and the churches sought to reach people in areas less touched by existing congregations. More recently, David Wasdell, working with the Urban Church Project in the 1970s, played a key part in reigniting interest in church planting, identifying the vital principle that more people go to church when there are more churches. This encouraged fresh activity, seen, for example, in the DAWN (Discipling a Whole Nation) movement, which aimed to set up 20,000 new churches across the country by the year 2000.

The recognition that more people will be reached through having more churches was right, but that was only part of the equation. Increasing numbers of churches that were basically simpler and less formal replicas of existing ones was not the answer in itself. The next stage, spurred by the inspiration of the *Mission-Shaped Church* report,[3] provided a remarkable injection of energy. The key was in grasping the need for contextualization, in listening to the local setting and shaping the church so that the unchanging gospel can be communicated and celebrated in ways that resonate with local culture. If that culture is geographically local, a sensitive parish church may be able to relate very well to all of its surrounding population, but often there will be different groups of people across a given area, each with distinctive

106

the unchanging gospel

interests, patterns of life, ways of communicating and networks of relationship.

This energy and impetus inspired by *Mission-Shaped Church* has been channelled by the Fresh Expressions organization,[4] set up by the Archbishops of Canterbury and York and the Methodist Council in 2004, to encourage the Fresh Expressions movement across all denominations. The Fresh Expressions website gives the following formal definition of a fresh expression of church:

- A fresh expression is a form of church for our changing culture, established primarily for the benefit of people who are not yet members of any church.
- It will come into being through principles of listening, service, incarnational mission and making disciples.
- It will have the potential to become a mature expression of church shaped by the gospel and the enduring marks of the church and for its cultural context.[5]

In other words, fresh expressions of church are fresh, deliberately shaped to communicate with and grow among people who are not currently part of church culture. But they are nevertheless expressions of church, identified with the Church of God and having the explicit aim of becoming self-governing, self-financing and self-replicating churches themselves. In terms of leadership, it means that there need to be people able to listen, pray, think and act on their feet. As one pioneering leader put it: 'I'm very intuitive and I'm an opportunist.' Leaders need to have a vision for what might be, faith to believe it can happen, and openness to welcome God's changes and surprises en route.

Through formal training, networking and sharing stories, the idea of fresh expressions has spread with remarkable speed. It has the sense of being a movement for which the time has come. The results, only a very few years after the concept began to be understood and accepted across the churches, are nothing short of remarkable. Across the Church of England, the dioceses surveyed so far record attendance at fresh expressions in a range from 4.4 per cent in Chelmsford to 16 per cent in Canterbury, with an average figure of just under 10 per cent being reflected across the country as research extends to further parts of the Church of England.[6]

Looking more closely at the figures, it is clear that fresh expressions of church have the potential to continue growing. They have shown themselves to draw people who either have no church background or lost contact with church some time ago, with leaders reporting 75 per cent falling into this category. Very few 'standard' churches – or 'inherited mode' churches, in the terminology usually employed by those involved in fresh expressions – seem able to attract anything like that proportion of people from outside the Christian community. Once a pattern of growth is established, it becomes normal and expected. Fresh expressions, set up with mission at their heart and with a high proportion of people who have recently come to faith, have, as it is frequently put in this context, a different 'DNA' from established churches. Growth, mission, flexibility and cultural relevance are accepted as key values by all involved, and communicated explicitly and implicitly in all that the new church does.

Fresh expressions are young, not only in terms of being new, flexible and unhindered by habit and tradition, although that is certainly a huge advantage. They are also young in terms of the age of their attenders, with an average of over 40 per cent of those attending being below the age of 16.[7] Portsmouth Diocese, home of Messy Church, records a remarkable 50.8 per cent of fresh expressions attenders being under 16. These figures are all the more noteworthy when we recognize that some fresh expressions deliberately focus on retired people and include no young people at all.

Fresh expressions are likely to continue growing partly due to the younger age profile and their attitude to mission. Their numerical significance within their host denominations has been developing at an increasing rate and there is no reason to expect that this trend will change. As a general rule, it is true to say that the most effective way of encouraging church growth is to establish new churches. Those new churches may actually take the form of new congregations of an existing church, but the point is that they are not clones, but have life, relevance and direction of their own, and are rooted in their context rather than being part of a separate and more 'churchy' culture.

Fresh expressions: unqualified good news?

Given the scale of growth across fresh expressions of church, and noting that a considerable proportion of that growth represents people coming afresh or returning to church, rather than a reloca-tion of existing Christians, there is clearly a great deal to celebrate. Initial fears on the part of some that fresh expressions would simply attract people seeking the new away from existing churches do not seem to be borne out by the research done so far. Further research by the Church Army, as yet unpublished, is focused on interviews with attenders at fresh expressions – the 2013 study recorded the views of leaders only – who seem to be reporting higher levels of previous church membership than had been thought, but the proportion of people attending with no previous church involvement is still high.

This is a movement that genuinely is making new disciples, not simply providing a refuge for disenchanted or experience-seeking Christians. Interestingly, not all fresh expressions show high levels of growth.[8] So-called 'alternative worship', exploring liturgy, music, art and creativity in new and imaginative ways, often attracting those who are already – perhaps disenchanted – church members, is an approach that shows low levels of continued growth. A large proportion of those groups grow and then decline, as the experience being sought fails to provide long-term satisfaction.

It is also worth noting that one other category of fresh expres-sions seems to have a tendency to grow up quickly but then to shrivel, perhaps because it does not have natural roots in our culture. Cell church groups represent the largest proportion of settings where initial growth is followed by shrinkage. Having been actively promoted by certain church planters in the 1990s, cell church seems to struggle outside the Global South. There may be cases, for example in rural areas, where cell-sized communities are the only available option, but a strategy that sees cell-based growth as a good thing per se would seem to be mistaken.

On the other hand, a longer look at the place of fresh expressions in the life of the whole Church points to another potential paradox. Is the very vibrancy and success of fresh expressions stifling life elsewhere in the Church? We will need to ponder that carefully; we explore some of these questions below, before going on to give some pointers as to how the Church in its inherited mode can grow and flourish alongside the multiplying fresh expressions of its life.

Does the inclusion in total church attendance statistics of involvement with fresh expressions mask the shocking scale of overall church decline?

As we examined in Chapter 1, attendance at churches in the mainstream denominations in Britain has shown a pattern of gentle but persistent decline since the 1950s, running at a rate of about 1 per cent decline per year. Within this general trend, the growth of fresh expressions of church has been a source of considerable encouragement. However, one clear conclusion to draw from the headline figures is stark: without fresh expressions, the overall scale of decline would be very significantly worse. Regular attendance at worship at 'standard' churches has been in virtual free-fall in some areas. This is compounded further by the reality of the age profile of inherited mode church. The younger – usually very significantly younger – age range of those involved in fresh expressions again masks the full picture with regard to the remainder of the Church. Without fresh expressions, the Church of England and quite probably the Methodist Church and other traditional denominations are far older and declining more rapidly than the headline figures alone would indicate.   Was Jesus measured by attendance?

Have fresh expressions taken the energy, vision and leadership gifts out of inherited mode church?

Some Christians are instinctive pioneers and entrepreneurs. Their deep, God-given desire is to be directing their energy and imagination towards doing new things, going where none has gone before. These were the people who built mission halls in new housing areas in the first half of the twentieth century, who chartered trains to take whole communities to hear Billy Graham at his crusade meetings, who persuaded their local church to try the Alpha course and then invited their neighbours to make sure that there was a crowd ready to join it. In each generation the instinctive missionaries will work in the way that is appropriate to their culture and setting, and their role is vital.

A growing proportion of those people with gifts in mission are now focusing their energies in fresh expressions of church. While traditional churches have changed significantly since the mid-twentieth century, society has changed yet faster. For those with a burning missionary heart, the opportunity to reach out in new ways – without the inertia created by church structures and without the cultural gulf between new disciples and traditional church – is understandably attractive. But once that energy and vision are lost to the bulk of churches, there is a very real danger that as fresh expressions multiply so other churches of a more traditional nature will be without the gifts and imagination they badly need.

While the Church Army research indicates that fresh expressions are not simply transferring people from existing congregations, the relatively limited quantitative loss may conceal a far greater removal of quality from church life. Those who remain may be faithful believers, but with less confidence and less drive than might otherwise be the case.

Given the imagination revealed in fresh expressions, is it easier for the Church as a whole to dodge the challenge of change across the board?

Entrepreneurs and pioneers can be people who are short on patience, who may tire of arguing at a deacons' meeting that the church chairs could all be moved out for a youth event, even if it has never been done before, or of working to persuade the organist to play anything by Graham Kendrick. If an opportunity arises to be in a different setting where there are fewer barriers to getting on with the work of mission, that's where the energy of these people will be focused.

prophetic witness

Losing the innovators, missionaries and prophets may, of course, be a great relief to some existing congregations. The need to change will seem less pressing. This will be in part because those pressing for change are able to direct their energies elsewhere, but it may also mean that a local church will be able to cite 'their' local fresh expression as evidence that they are indeed reaching out in new ways. Since new things are happening somewhere close by, there is less urgency about creating anything new in the 'proper' church. The DNA of inherited mode churches does not have the same natural willingness to embrace change for the sake of mission, and is unlikely to change if the movers and shakers have left. The forlorn refrain, 'We want to attract more young families but we don't want to change the way we do things' may well continue to be expressed.

It is telling that the *Mission-Shaped Church* report, in Graham Cray's introduction, discusses extensively the significance of different specific contexts. The next chapter, 'Changing Contexts', goes on to identify significant trends that affect the whole of British society. The context of change is the whole nation. By implication, context-specific churches cannot only be those set up to relate to new settings. If the entire national context is in the process of rapid and continued change, every church in the country needs to examine how it relates to its context, and to recognize that there will need to be change, at least of some kind, in the light of that exploration.

The Anglican–Methodist report *Fresh Expressions in the Life of the Church*[9] provides an overview of the movement. It was written in the main by people who were not practitioners in establishing fresh expressions, and their view, interestingly, became more positive in the process of writing, as each undertook to spend time in at least one fresh expression. A significant and helpful insight in the report is the comment:

> The transition from neighbourhood to network society, though a recognizable phenomenon, should not be overstated. As yet, few people inhabit a purely network society. In practice, communities are formed through a combination of neighbourhood and social networks.[10]

the inherited church was once a content church

INHERITED MODE You have heard it said...

But I say to you...

There is strength and wisdom in mutual understanding, and in acknowledging that we are in a period of transition that will allow space for a range of models of interrelationship between Church and society. Churches relating to networks and geographical areas are both needed, and each needs to appreciate the interplay and overlap between them.

Free-standing fresh expressions can struggle to survive

When I was diocesan missioner, the Diocese of Lichfield began to address its failure to reach young adults in the 18–30 age group and embarked on an ambitious plan to plant a series of network-based churches to reach young adults in some of the urban conurbations of the diocese. Money was found from various sources and four exceptionally gifted and able pioneers (three ordained, one lay) were recruited, to work full time as church planters. Each was sent and deployed as a solitary worker. Attempts were made at an early stage to find partners who would form a core team around each pioneer, but this proved elusive in most cases. Ten years on, the fruit of these four projects in terms of new disciples has been very modest; none of them has become anything like able to support a full-time stipendiary priest, and the three clergy have gone back into parish ministry – where, interestingly, some are see-ing more people come to faith than they did in their 'pioneer' roles. For each of them, their experience as a pioneer minister was quite a draining and lonely one.

Reflecting on the experience, I think perhaps we went about it the wrong way. Instead of starting by finding funding and employing a stipendiary pioneer, I wonder if we should have begun by seeking out local people with a heart for that com-munity who would covenant to meet together to pray, and gradually form a praying community. Only as a praying com-munity started to emerge on the ground should we have begun to ask what kind of leadership was appropriate and how we could pay for it.

One of those pioneer priests, looking back on the experience, comments:

> When the solo pioneers got together we often wondered what might have happened if the Diocese had put more of its eggs in one basket. What if it had at least sent us two by two, or even placed us all together . . . from a much stronger start maybe we could have replicated good practice through all the regional centres we were called to. I have absolutely no regrets in doing this role, but know that without even the fledgling team I gathered nothing could have happened.

Launching out alone in mission is a lonely experience. Even St Paul, stepping out with the Christian message for the very first time in Asia Minor, took with him at least one companion. Most fresh expressions have started with a small team, the great majority being between three and 12 people.[11] That's not a big crowd to take on the task, especially if one overall leader is the main keeper of the vision. In the end, pressing on without clear and effective links to the wider Church can be draining. As one pioneer put it in conversation, 'Everything always comes back to me.'

Initial responses to the Church Army's investigation of those attending fresh expressions seem to give some support to these conclusions. They indicate that a significant number of people involved in fresh expressions also have a link with another congregation. Interestingly, multiple congregations in large church settings stand out as the form of fresh expression most likely to show sustained growth and least likely to decline.[12] This model is, by definition, not available in small church settings. It may also have the advantage of gifted leadership already in place, and the back-up of office facilities and publicity. However, it may well be that the clear link with an existing church is part of the strength of this model, even as it aims to establish a new and separate identity. The need for a connection with 'standard' church is being recognized by many people, even as they launch out in new ways beyond the existing churches.

Fresh expressions of church will not pay the bills

Regular attenders at long-established churches will be well aware that they are expensive to maintain. Cold, leaky buildings are not easy to ignore, and fundraising is a way of life for many congregations. It is also likely that people who are fully involved in the life of inherited mode churches will have at least some understanding of the need for structures beyond the local setting. Cathedrals, bishops, regional offices and regional officers all cost money, and long-established congregations will recognize this, albeit reluctantly. Traditional churchgoers, used to the presence of a vicar or minister in vicarage or manse, will also have an understanding of the cost of this.

In contrast to the traditional pattern, many fresh expressions of church meet outside church buildings, perhaps in school halls or community centres, sometimes in private homes. Those that use church premises – for example, in a multiple congregation setting – may well have fewer people among their membership who exercise leadership roles in the whole church, and less grasp of the full scale of costs involved. More significantly, a significant proportion – initial research by the Church Army suggests 40 per cent in Anglican settings – of fresh expressions are led by 'lay-lay' people – that is, ordinary church members who are neither ordained, licensed nor formally trained. In other denominations they are usually referred to as 'Christians'!

New believers, excited by the message of Jesus Christ, and wanting to respond financially, will recognize the need to cover the costs of the group within which they have encountered faith. But if that group has no expensive building, no significant training outlay for the leaders, no salaries to pay and little link with the wider diocese or denomination, it will be a tall order to convince new believers that a significant proportion of their giving should go to support a high-cost, inherited church structure.

There may be cheers from many of those reading these words. We do not want to imply that fresh attitudes to financial priorities are a bad thing – it may be exactly what the Church needs. The message is simply that fresh expressions are not going to be the source of financial salvation for denominations or dioceses. But then again, the salvation Jesus offered was never intended to be financial.

Holding on to a vision for 'both and' in the life of the Church

The paradox of flourishing fresh expressions alongside struggling inherited mode churches need not prove insoluble. There are real grounds for seeing both fresh expressions and inherited mode church as part of a healthy and positive future. If understanding and respect between the two is enabled to grow, both have an important part to play in the next stage of the Church's life in Britain. The future needs to be one in which that respect and mutual understanding will be increasingly significant.

Keeping a firm commitment to fresh expressions

The speed at which fresh expressions of church have expanded over the last 15 years has been quite remarkable. From being the preserve of a small number of enthusiasts, new ventures are starting up at an increasing rate. As discussed, the Church Army study of ten dioceses across the Church of England in 2013 revealed a clear pattern of accelerated growth after 2003 (see Figure 8.1), and the *Mission-Shaped Church* report clearly had an immediate and sustained impact upon practice.

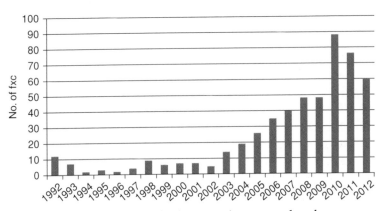

Figure 8.1 The number of fresh expressions started each year between 1992 and 2012 across ten Church of England dioceses[13]

Figure 8.1 also indicates the first signs of a levelling off in the rate of increase. This is not entirely certain, since the 2012 data are incomplete and the report suggests that a likely level of 80 for that year may be more accurate. Even allowing for this, the pattern seems to indicate a slowing in expansion, but it is still at a far higher level than ten or 12 years before. In other words, fresh expressions of church are now an established reality, playing an increasingly important part in the life of the Church of England and of the Methodist Church, which shares in the Fresh Expressions initiative. While the movement looks unlikely to expand exponentially and replace existing patterns of church life in the short term, it can no longer be seen as a minority interest for enthusiasts.

While a remarkable range of fresh expressions is now in existence,[14] not all those involved in establishing and leading them will be the most highly gifted pioneers. Early adopters are following the innovators, and this will need recognition and support, since adopters will not have the vision, flexibility and courage of the most inspired innovators. As imaginative and visionary leaders are joined by good and competent successors, the need for support from para-church organizations, from dioceses and from denominations will become increasingly important. This is evident in a number of areas, but two stand out.

First, there is a need to keep the imagination open. The bulk of recent fresh expressions are in the category of either café church or Messy Church. Both are important, and fit well into current mainstream culture. We will look at Messy Church more closely in the next chapter. If one challenge to Messy Church is to make sure it stays messy, perhaps the task for those involved in establishing fresh expressions is to keep thinking in fresh ways. There is a danger that some of the hard work of paying attention to local culture, listening to God and grappling prayerfully with where that leads can drop out of the process if there are easily adopted models of fresh expressions available nearby. Increased awareness of where and how fresh expressions work best will make it easier to target settings with obvious potential for growth. But God is not concerned only with the obvious, and people living in settings and communities where growth is likely to be difficult to achieve matter every bit as much in God's sight. Those guiding and inspiring the Fresh Expressions movement will need to work hard to keep it truly fresh.

Second, there is a need to support those leading fresh expressions, and to encourage continued growth, particularly perhaps as the first burst of energy on the part of the start-up team may start to flag. This is in large measure a new movement, and most fresh expressions of church are still in the early stages of becoming established. The support needs will also increase as exceptional pioneers are followed by others. Early successes and strong evidence of growth should not be interpreted as showing that growing fresh expressions is easy. The first ventures by inspirational leaders had less support available, but also probably needed less, given the calibre of some of the leaders we have spoken to. As understanding and expertise grow across the country, it is essential that that knowledge is made available to the growing range of fresh expressions and those leading them.

Keeping different expressions of church in touch with one another

One leader of a new church that is bringing together women with no previous church involvement told of how the women in the group had heard that Christians did something with bread and wine. She introduced them to Holy Communion, along with icons and candles. The symbols and actions of the historic Church resonated with a new generation in a hired hall, and a number of new believers have been baptized as the church has grown. As the Bishop put it, 'You believe in all the sacraments, but not necessarily in the right order!'

There is much wisdom in the experience of the historic Church, and in the life experience of members of established denominations. There has never been a church that is not contextualized, but generations of church members have been unaware of that reality. As long as established churches view themselves as 'normal', the flexibility of thought needed to work with fresh expressions to understand together how strengths can be shared will not be present. The more long-standing congregations and ministers accept that they are only one part, albeit a significant part, of what God is doing, the more it may become natural for questions of church, faith, context, culture and mission to be shared in all directions. Both old and new will be strengthened in the process.

Welcoming a new reality

There is no going back. Alongside the established denominations, fresh expressions of church have grown up and are now a significant presence. From being the preserve of pioneers and enthusiasts, they now comprise a significant proportion of worshipping Christians. Every indicator points to an increasing numerical significance of fresh expressions relative to the size of established congregations.

In highlighting one way towards rapid growth and developing worshipping communities in parts of society previously untouched, fresh expressions of church are increasingly shining a spotlight on existing church life, where cultural relevance may be less and growth harder to find. They oblige the whole Church to examine what real growth in discipleship, as opposed to drawing people into church culture, may look like. Also, with the avoidance of many of the trappings of traditional church life, important considerations of which traditions and practices are actually of great value are opened up, and how they can be woven into the experience of new Christian communities. On the other hand, the wisdom of years and the established faith found in inherited mode churches should not be too quickly dismissed. The experience of the early years of this century would seem to indicate a best way forward in which the newer and older models of church work alongside each other, with the serious task of mutual understanding, learning and respect being given a high priority.

So does inherited mode church still have a place? Specifically in the case of the Church of England, can parish churches continue to be effective bases for mission in their communities?

We believe they can, although the pretence that one Sunday service can serve all sections of the population within that parish needs to be relinquished. After looking closer at Messy Church in the next chapter, we will go on to ponder how inherited mode churches can still play their part effectively in making new disciples.

9

Messy Church: Messy enough? Church enough?

————◆•◆•◆————

Beginnings are always messy. (John Galsworthy)

When we were surveying the growing range of materials and resources available for churches during the writing of *EWWN* (2003), we took a step back and realized something significant. Nothing of national significance seemed to have its main focus on reaching children and families. At a time when the impact of ageing on the profile of congregations was beginning to be clear, the main direction people were exploring as they looked to the future seemed to have almost no concern for the generations who would be at the heart of that future. With a degree of alarm, we wrote:

> The fall-off in work among children is one of the most serious pieces of news for the Church in contemporary Britain. Adopting new strategies for evangelism while leaving children's work untouched is simply postponing disaster. To have hope for the future there needs to be hope in that generation that will become the future.[1]

Unknown to us at the time, God was already at work. Over the last decade, Messy Church has expanded across the life of the Church, involving most denominations, in a way that is reminiscent of the early expansion of Alpha some years ago. Like Alpha, it appears to be suited to the moment. Also like Alpha, Messy Church has emerged in a UK context, and seems able to take root naturally in a way that new insights that have come from across the Atlantic or other parts of the world have found harder to achieve.

The Messy Church website introduces the movement:

The first Messy Church began in 2004 when a group at St Wilfrid's in Cowplain near Portsmouth were frustrated because, as a church, we were hardly reaching any children with God's story ... We decided very early on to try to do something for all ages together, partly out of a belief that we grow best as a church when we walk the journey with as many different people as possible, and partly from a desire to help families grow together in their walk of faith, not see Christianity as something you grow out of when you're eleven.[2]

In the years since then, Messy Church has grown and flourished with remarkable speed. The Bible Reading Fellowship[3] keeps records of those Messy Churches registered with the national network, and currently the number has passed 2,500, but a brief survey of my local area revealed several that are not yet registered, and this is likely to be true nationally. Clearly the movement is expanding at a pace that is going beyond easy recording.

The very name, Messy Church, sets out an important corrective to the perceptions of many people about church worship. Churches are seen as places where one should be well behaved and tidy, where noise is to be kept to a minimum. When, after a recent funeral, a small reception was held in my home church that included a bottle of whisky, I was asked by a curious – or possibly anxious – member of the congregation, 'So, were you happy with it happening *in church*?' Actions and behaviours accepted as perfectly normal outside church buildings or church gatherings are seen as questionable at the very least when church is involved. Many years ago, Archbishop William Temple was reported to have commented, 'The Church of England is dying of good taste.' Two generations later, little seems to have changed, and the Messy Church brand name and logo are designed to blow away that anxiety.

The messiness of Messy Church is not restricted to the range of craft activities or to children's table manners. There is, quite consciously, an open, messy, exploratory, interactive feel to the whole operation. Lucy Moore, founder of the movement, reports of its early days:

> We're not organized enough for questionnaires and surveys, but we're good chatters. We talked to people at the school gate. We walked dogs with them and listened. We talked about it to people in church and out of church and got a gut feeling and vision of what God might be trying to say to us.[4]

Messy Church as a movement is determinedly open-ended, with a sense of tapping into what is working without feeling the need to see exactly where it may all lead. The messiness is not only literal, although that is certainly important. It is a symbolic acceptance of a questing and informal approach both to faith and to the nature of the Church.

A typical Messy Church service

Welcome

Being welcomed at Messy Church may involve receiving a bag of goodies for use during the activities ahead, stopping for drinks and biscuits, or pausing to put on a name badge. It's not likely to be on a Sunday morning, since most Messy Churches meet after school on weekdays or around teatime on Saturdays or Sunday. Nor will it necessarily be in church. Often the starting point is in a hall, either church or community owned. Some meet in schools, although others have made a conscious decision to avoid a building associated with school work and rules. If it is in a church, the next hour or two will not involve much sitting on pews!

Exploration

After the theme has been introduced, the next section of the gathering is used to explore a story or idea from Scripture. There will be a range of craft ideas and games that seek to explore the theme, and people will move around to join in all or most of them. A story about God guiding us might be experienced through creating a maze, or belonging together through mixing ingredients to bake soda bread. Some are noisy, a few messy, many wonderfully ingenious, while some are quiet as people of all ages use a secluded corner to think and to pray. It's about involving all the senses, and takes place in the context of relationship, with people chatting together about the theme all through each activity, sharing insights, grappling with questions.

Celebration

This is the bit that looks most like a recognizable service. In some cases, the whole group processes to the church building to claim it as their worship space. If the same room as Exploration is used it will need some clear space so that people can move on without stopping to tidy everything up. The celebration is short, looking again at the Bible story that has been explored together, and bringing together the questions, hope and emotions generated. Some churches finish with a Messy grace, leading into the last and important part of each Messy meeting.

Food

Eating together as an all-age activity may be a novel experience for many in the middle of over-busy lives. It also allows for further conversation and sharing news of life as people catch up with each other and relax together.

The Messy difference

Many of the elements of Messy Church are by no means new. The presence of a shared meal has been identified as a key element in the success of Alpha.[5] More importantly, of course, Christian worship has its roots in eating together – the agape feast from which the bread and wine as central elements of the Eucharist became separated as the first generations of the Church progressed. Food at Messy Church is not an original idea, but it is certainly one with a very good pedigree.

All-age worship has also been part of church life for many years in various forms. The craft activities found in Messy settings are much like those used in a range of children's holiday clubs. The open and explorative nature of Messy Church is not unique either. It draws on principles also found in Godly Play,[6] an approach to work with children that uses open-ended and hands-on investigation to 'wonder' about the meaning and significance of the stories that make up the Christian tradition. Messy Church recognizes, with Godly Play, the validity of childhood faith, the importance of community and the value of exploration and non-directive learning. Some Messy Churches deliberately involve Godly Play activities in the range of options available, and the two can sit happily alongside each other. But they are noticeably different in feel. Messy Church is less controlled, more open to flexibility, and involves more food. It aims to reach those outside the Church, whereas Godly Play focuses on nurturing those within; Messy Church is less closely tied to existing patterns of church life and worship. Messy Church is frankly, well, just more *messy*.

Perhaps the most helpful way of explaining what Messy Church is, is to look more closely at what it *is not*.

- *Messy Church is not a club.* Some activities may be very similar to those on offer at summer holiday clubs, but the dynamic and purpose are decidedly different. Quite simply, Messy Church is a church. And this leads on to the next important point.
- *Messy Church is not a feeder into 'real' church.* Some people may be contacted initially through Messy Church, and then become increasingly involved in the supporting church or another local fellowship, but this is very definitely not the intention.
- *Messy Church is not a children's activity.* It aims to relate to all ages. Many will be in family groups, and indeed safeguarding and health and safety concerns are likely to mean that children must be supervised by parents or regular carers. But it is not only for families. Churches report the life-enhancing impact of belonging on older members, in particular, as they share in helping with food, with planning worship or with preparing materials for craft activities.

The Messy future and the future of discipleship

Messy Church gatherings are usually on a monthly, as opposed to weekly, basis. Given this fact, and the interactive nature of sessions – exploring the theme followed by only a brief act of shared worship – it is not surprising that the issue of how discipleship can grow in Messy Church has been regularly raised. It is interesting that those who come from outside the movement itself generally tend to point to ways of partnering, following on from or adding in other ways to Messy Church.

Voices from outside

A study by the Diocese of Lichfield[7] reported that 69 per cent of those attending Messy Church go to a Sunday family service at least occasionally. It enquires about the provision of nurture courses as a way of building on the Messy Church experience, but although 75 per cent of respondents have offered courses, take-up is relatively low, with only 65 of Messy Churches able to give a firm answer that some have attended the courses. The authors comment:

> We have come across one church where a significant number of people from Messy Church have gone to an Alpha course. We do wonder how many churches have been intentional in inviting personally their Messy contacts. For many of them, however, courses like Alpha would be too far along the faith path and many need a way of exploring pre-Alpha questions.[8]

Reasons for the low take-up may relate to most nurture courses taking place in the evening, when parents involved in Messy events with the whole family may find it hard to attend because of child-care arrangements. There is also a change of ethos, involving a move from an all-age to an adult-only environment: a challenging change for parents who may be more comfortable with the needs of the children being a stated reason for their attendance at an event.

The Lichfield report goes on to point out another significant challenge for any add-on activity associated with Messy Church.

Going to an event and joining in, it is only normal human nature to feel far more comfortable doing so if accompanied by someone who knows the setting and can take you with them. Invitation is a fundamental part of any evangelistic activity, and Messy Church leaders are likely to be so stretched in setting up and resourcing each monthly event that attendance at a nurture course with an interested Messy Church member may simply be too big a demand on their time.

Bob Jackson writes: 'Much more experimentation is needed to enable congregations formed around a monthly Messy Church to meet more often and grow spiritually as Christian communities.'[9] His suggestions include groups like 'Who let the dads out?' or a 'messy café' on weeks between main Messy gatherings.

Anglican Church Planting Initiatives (ACPI), writing on Messy Church, nurture and discipleship,[10] has a range of suggestions for 'deepening' the Messy Church context and, perhaps more usefully, for adding further to the monthly Messy meetings. Suggestions include providing resources for families to use in nurturing faith in the home, cell groups – including all-age cells – and parenting support groups. Other ideas, such as storytelling workshops, have the potential to build on the desire of those growing more deeply involved in the running of Messy Church to play their part as well, while giving fresh space to explore the theological meaning of the stories being told.

Perhaps most valuable in the ACPI list is the suggestion that Messy Church members are encouraged to get involved in social action projects. This can build on the culture of participation and exploration that is part of the messy world. It also gives power and authenticity to the stories of the actions of Jesus, as people share in his mission. In some cases, the shared meal in Messy Church already has a significant function in providing good food for families who perhaps struggle to feed themselves well. Purposeful engagement of Messy members with the Church's work for justice, peace and the common good may not add greatly to their theoretical knowledge, but could have a profound effect on their understanding of the significance of Jesus' teaching and of the power of the Holy Spirit as they see God at work.

More voices from inside

In acknowledging the thoughts and suggestions of those who have been pondering Messy Church and discipleship as outside observers, it is absolutely wrong to infer that the Messy Church movement and its practitioners are not already keenly aware of the challenge of discipleship. Lucy Moore has rightly commented on the discipleship deficit in most forms of church,[11] and would want to stress that this is most certainly not just a Messy Church issue. If critics of Messy Church point out that it is difficult to see how wholehearted discipleship can be nurtured by a church that meets only monthly, it is only honest to face the increasing reality of monthly attendance at 'standard' church. The difference is that Messy Church is *designed* to meet only monthly, and those overseeing the direction of a local church in this pattern can work in a deliberate way to weave monthly main meetings into whole-life pattern. Those who, by default, attend once a month at other churches may actually find themselves far less well served by a pattern of church life that still works on the assumption of weekly worship and continuity from one week to the next.

The lack of frequent churchy activities within Messy Church need not prevent people growing more like Jesus. The particular strength of Messy Church, when working well, is relationship. A monthly gathering where people of all ages spend a significant proportion of their time in discussion or shared activity can produce far deeper mutual understanding than several weeks of pew-sitting.

Moreover, if discipleship is seen as a means of conforming people to an existing church pattern, it may not necessarily be primarily about becoming more like Jesus, and thus may produce church members but not disciples.[12] So what, then, are the main elements of discipleship identified by those at the heart of Messy Church? The first is a determined attachment to all-age learning and growth. This is fundamental to the main Messy gathering. A recent tool to encourage ongoing growth in faith, Messy Lyfe,[13] is specifically aimed at being child-led, providing a series of studies for the whole family group, with the expectation that children will take the lead in initiating discussion.

While commendable in recognizing how generations depend on one another, and in particular that children can enable adults to grow spiritually (after all, Jesus did say that receiving the kingdom like a little child was normative for all ages[14]), this approach may not do justice to the reality of life experience. Even for busy parents, significant parts of life will be dominated by issues of work, sexuality, finance, politics and other topics that cannot easily be addressed in an all-age setting. Childlike trust in God still needs to be exercised in adult situations that are both complex and inappropriate for discussion by children, and there is a need for adult-only space in which to address this.

The second striking element of discussion about discipleship by committed Messy practitioners is the breathless excitement about growth and newness. To those involved it can feel as though they are at the stage of removing stones and preparing the ground for sowing, and so language of growth and approaching maturity may seem very premature. Many of those joining Messy Church have almost no awareness of the fundamentals of the Christian message, and even less experience of church practices and culture. The overwhelming experience is one of welcoming and beginning to develop relationships, of starting things up, seeing things at an early stage and being thrilled by growth rather than being overly troubled about where it may all lead in ten years' time. These are simply not the elements of life found in the great bulk of existing churches, and discussion about discipleship can sometimes seem a dialogue of the deaf, with observers outside Messy Church asking questions that originate in a very different church setting. Meanwhile, those caught up in the life and excitement of Messy Church feel themselves to be at a far earlier, open and fluid stage in church building.

The discussion of discipleship from the perspective of Messy Church enthusiasts is live and active, though currently still in its early days.

Some questions for Messy Church

Faith and 'the faith'

Pondering the remarkable, energizing and inspiring phenomenon that is Messy Church, a number of paradoxes emerge. The first is the interaction between faith and 'the faith'. What elements of the faith, as passed down through the centuries, are of such importance that they really do need to be included, one way or another, in the Messy experience? Engaging with Messy Church at its best leaves no space for doubt that faith is being exercised, tested, grown and shared. But individual faith is just one part of the faith of the Church, shaped and tested through history. It is far easier, for example, to explore the teaching and actions of Jesus or the stories of the Old Testament in a Messy way. Grappling with Paul's epistles, and specifically with the doctrinal teaching that underlies the practical advice usually found in the later part of the letters, will be far less straightforward. But if the faith is truly to be encountered, those who are becoming disciples of Jesus will need to be able to learn from the greatest disciples who have gone before them and left their teaching as a gift to those who will follow.

Bringing together the growing faith expressed in many Messy Churches with 'the faith' will inevitably then lead to the question of how the sacraments may best be expressed within Messy Church. Simply pointing people to 'proper' church when they wish to enquire about baptism or to receive communion goes directly against the conviction that Messy Church is indeed church, not an outreach activity. A number of Messy Churches have hosted baptism services for infants, children and adults. As long as the wider family of those to be baptized is ready to dispense with some expectations of what a baptism might involve, there is scope for this to be one of the high points in the life of a Messy congregation.

Holy Communion has proved far more difficult to integrate. Although the Salvation Army – which does not have Holy Communion as part of its worship – is well represented in Messy Church nationally, the great bulk of Messy Churches are linked to denominations and networks that do share communion. And yet with the integration of a shared meal into every gathering, Messy Church is already profoundly eucharistic, with various elements of communion present and celebrated each month. Perhaps the way forward is for Messy Church, joyfully and without inhibition, to launch into full-on Messy Communions. Liturgical rules will be almost impossible to follow, and all sorts of people of all ages will be as welcome as were the tax collectors and sinners who dined with Jesus. A number of churches, perhaps especially the Church of England, will struggle to find ways of fitting what is happening into existing regulations, but maybe the whole Church of God will discover new truths about just what Jesus intended when he said to his followers, 'Do this to remember me.'

Staying fresh as we all grow older

How will Messy Church survive as children grow older? Can it be cool enough for teenagers? How can it respond when young people have a natural developmental need to establish their identity in a way that is less closely tied to the relationship with their parents? One of the most impressive Messy Churches we contacted had a major focus on growing young leaders. Young people from Year 6 (ages 10–11) were involved not simply as assistants when the church met but in the planning, praying and preparation in the intervening weeks. In exploring Scripture together, grappling with its meaning and working through questions together before practical activities were considered, serious theological work was being done. The close personal relationship with adult leaders allowed for godly living and thinking to be modelled. There is scope for an ongoing transition to full leadership roles, but if the best way forward is to establish a youth group centred on young people with that level of theological awareness and experience of responsibility, what grows may then prove to be even more exciting.

Staying messy in a tidy world

In exploring a number of groups around the eastern part of the England, we were struck by the sense that things could sometimes be a bit messier! There is a danger that Messy Church can actually become Craft Church. Messiness, in terms of things exploding, creating enormous coloured puddles on the floor or flying around the room at great speed, is actually quite hard to keep going. Settling into a pattern of craft activity, especially when leaders may have specific skills they are eager to use, can allow some of the freshness to fade.

Craft activities can be engrossing for some, but others may lack manual skills and hence feel short of confidence. Men are often in a minority in churches, and one likely reason for this is unease at singing in our current cultural context. Messy Church, in focusing on craft activities, may be in danger of providing another turn-off to the male half of the population. The study by Lichfield Diocese[15] reports fewer boys than girls in Messy Church, and most of our visits to Messy Churches seemed to confirm this pattern. One church near Cambridge has responded by making sure that there is always a specific technology activity available at each month's gathering, and this regularly attracts a mainly male group. Yet the answer may actually be more straightforward: if there is one thing most boys love (speaking as a father and grandfather of boys, with some rather good memories of being a boy myself), it's *mess*. Dedicated leaders with craft skills to share, churchwardens, deacons or stewards with a concern for the well-being of buildings, and parents with washing to think about, can all collude to make Messy Church a bit too neat. This should be resisted, and Messy Church needs to keep working hard to stay true to its messy self.

The Messy Church website has specific (if brief) resources on ideas for activities that may specifically appeal to boys,[16] and links to the wonderfully named (but sadly defunct) Sweaty Church in York. While sport and active learning are not male preserves, of course, Sweaty Church took Messy inspirations and applied them to sports and activity, specifically aiming to be a place where those who learn though action – kinaesthetic learners – can flourish as they encounter Jesus. If traditional churches are dominated by the demand to sit still and be quiet – hard enough for children, and most adults too, but maybe especially for boys – even detailed craft activity may not hold everyone's attention, and Sweaty Church provides an excellent, if currently discontinued, example of Messy principles being transferable and, it is hoped, made more accessible to boys.

Being local but belonging to a movement

One particularly freshening element of the whole Messy project is the openness to local experimentation. In the first book on Messy Church, Lucy Moore specifically invites people to take up the principles and to use them in other ways. Rather than creating clones across the country, the inspiration is clearly laid out in a way that can be shared, owned, modified, reworked and used to grow new things suited to their context.

A few people have taken up this challenge. A small network with the name of Mossy Church is working with the same principles to explore faith in a creation-centred way.[17] Until recently, Sweaty Church in York worked with similar principles to integrate Messy approaches with sport. But overall, the great majority of local expressions of Messy inspiration are following the Messy Church recipe fairly closely.

So why, given the open invitation to experiment, are so many local groups adopting a remarkably similar pattern, with craft activities as the main focus? There is certainly value in brand recognition, and as Messy Church is spreading rapidly, the name and distinctive red logo on posters and materials give an immediate message about what to expect. But probably the main reason for the great majority of local groups staying close to the original recipe is that laying on multiple activity options each month takes a huge amount of time and imagination. Messy Church is not an easy option. Many hours of preparation are usually involved, and even when leaders are both gifted and imaginative, the back-up of a national network to share ideas and a growing range of published resources can be a life-saver. Branching out in a completely new direction will take not only imagination but also long-term creativity if the venture is to be sustained, and it may be that an exceptional figure will have to emerge before that can be a reality. In the meantime, dropping in to your local Messy Church will be great fun, but perhaps just a little predictable.

Working with families but reaching all ages

Visiting Messy Churches can be a slightly awkward experience for a single man. In seeking to be child-friendly, and in consciously targeting families, Messy Church is not an easy place for outsiders to drop in when they are not linked to a family. There is most certainly a need for everyone, including single people and older people, to be fully involved in supporting Messy Church and helping it all to happen – there's a lot to be done each month. But it is probably never going to be the place where any significant number of adults or couples without children will come to explore faith.

Recognizing that Messy Church is targeted at families is not in any sense a criticism. Untargeted ventures in church life regularly fail to reach anyone at all. But any local group launching into Messy Church will need to know that this cannot be a strategy for reaching every part of the local population. The most effective Messy Churches know that what they are doing is just one part of God's work, and the thriving Messy Churches we contacted were deeply involved in a range of other ways in their communities. Messy Church grows best when the local church and local Christians are known and respected, and when there is already an awareness that the Church is good news. In other words, Messy Church is most definitely church, not a way into church, but it is seldom likely to be the sum total of church in a given area. The whole population is wider than children and families, and children and families themselves will gain more from relating to a whole church that aims to share Jesus with all parts of the community in which it resides.

The Feast

Reydon, a village in Suffolk, is working with an impressive variant of Messy Church, known as The Feast. A monthly family service that often attracted no children was badly in need of a rethink. The Feast emerged, still meeting on a Sunday but starting with breakfast. Acknowledging from the start that most of those who are part of The Feast will be only monthly attenders, the aim has been to provide a welcome for all ages. Along with craft activities and Godly Play, there is always an opportunity to take time in serious Bible study. Other options include Table Talk, a discussion of the Sunday papers, and Nooma DVDs. Those attending do not always divide according to age – children sometimes join in Bible study and adults often go for craft – but there is a conscious intention that people of all ages, and not only those with families, will be welcomed and able to participate fully alongside each other.

It is easy to criticize Messy Church. The limitations of its scope for outreach and potential for focused adult teaching are obvious. But in the face of questions and critiques, Messy Church has been growing by leaps and bounds over the last decade and more. The main and repeated response of those practitioners asked to comment is, 'It works!' While nobody, least of all those at the heart of Messy Church as a movement, would claim that it is the sole answer to the challenges facing the Church in the UK, it most certainly is part of the answer, and a part that is well matched to the current time and setting. In establishing one particular way of outworking Messy principles, Messy Church is explicit that this is not a narrow, tightly controlled movement. From the start, the invitation to others has been there to take the inspiration and concept and to develop it further, in new ways and new settings. When that starts to happen on a significant scale, there will almost certainly be more chapters and more books to be written.

Is it because raising children is now a subset in the larger culture

10

Parish: mature or stale?

———•◦•———

When I'm on stage, I'm trying to do one thing: bring
people joy. Just like church does. People don't go to
church to find trouble: they go there to lose it.

(James Brown)

Maintaining confidence in inherited mode church

Having considered the growth of fresh expressions of church and
looked closely at Messy Church, what hope is there for the remainder of the Church? Does church in inherited mode have a future?
We believe that, alongside fresh expressions, there remains huge
potential for inherited mode church to play its part in reaching
every part of society with the Christian message.

First, and perhaps not obvious to everyone, traditional churches
have buildings, and buildings can speak when nobody else can
begin the conversation. While large and leaking structures can be
a burden, they also, by their very existence, present a huge opportunity. The presence of the Church in architecture makes a statement about the historic place of Christianity in our national life.
Yes, it is a mixed message, speaking sometimes of dominance and
control as church spires loom over surrounding housing, but the
physical presence of church buildings has the potential to make
Christianity available. Older buildings, imbued with the prayer of
centuries, can have their own spiritual power. Churchyards draw
many who are working with grief and treasuring memories.

Going with the Gothic

Old, atmospheric buildings can be used in mission not in spite
of their fascinating and slightly creepy nature but because of

it. One of the best events for young people in our local churches recently was a 'Do you dare spend the night with the bats?' sleepover in the church building. In the young adult novel *Shadowmancer*, the description of the author, the Anglican priest G. P. Taylor, could even be applied to clergy to make their role sound altogether more exciting: 'G. P. Taylor has spent the whole of his life searching for the hidden secrets of the universe. He lectures on the paranormal and folklore and lives in a secluded graveyard.'[1]

Newer, more flexible church centres can allow for a huge range of community activities, each with the potential for living and communicating the good news. Those who have spent hours walking up and down outside a hired building, praying that it will be available the next month for a new congregation to meet in, will know how vulnerable fresh expressions of church can be if their building needs are dependent on the goodwill of others.

Alongside visible buildings, visible clergy, active in the life of the local community, present an ongoing opportunity for enquirers to initiate conversations. The minister in the clerical collar may not know how many times his or her presence in the community has raised questions, how often people have 'nearly' spoken. The old model of full-time minister and church building is costly to maintain, but has the huge advantage of visibility. It allows people in the vicinity to know that the church is *there*; in part it is the source of that instinct that the church – which usually means the church building – is the place to go when a crisis hits.

Tim Alban Jones tells the story of the local church's place in one specific crisis, in Soham in Cambridgeshire.

When two schoolgirls, Holly and Jessica, went missing in August 2002 no one could have imagined how events would unfold. Within a week, the town of Soham and the parish church of St Andrew's was in the middle of a media whirlwind. We were inundated with reporters from all over the world; what was a private family tragedy soon became a national and then international event.

The church quickly became a focus for the community, providing space for people to come and pray; to write messages of condolence; to bring flowers, light a candle; or simply be together. The church was able to provide a valuable ministry by making the building available and to staff it with volunteers who could listen to visitors and pray with them.

The Church has both the architecture and the vocabulary to be able to deal with difficult events such as the tragedy in Soham, or any loss and bereavement. Merely by being open and available – by being there – for people, the parish church is able to achieve far more than it realizes.

Getting to know the life of any local church will soon reveal a band, although sometimes a shrinking one, of exceptionally dedicated churchwardens, stewards, elders, children's workers, cleaners, musicians, prayer warriors and others. The job descriptions may vary between denominations but the commitment is the same. Often they belong to the generation that lived through a world war, and know what it is to rebuild afterwards. They may not be those best suited to establishing fresh expressions of church, but their example can be an inspiration to team members who perhaps need reminding that building a church calls for dedicated hard work. Some of the older generation, especially, will have a commitment to prayer that is both a support and an example to younger people involved in new ventures.

The Church in its inherited forms, across many denominations and different traditions, is a vast repository of practical wisdom and lived theology. It has depths of resources that will continue to be of great importance to the life of the nation. Yes, those who are reaching out in new ways through fresh expressions may need to develop the agility to draw on and communicate afresh those depths and that wisdom, but that may be part of the potential for creative mutual understanding and support, which we will look at below.

Breathing fresh life into inherited mode church

While fresh expressions have been expanding rapidly, it would be wrong to suggest that nothing has been going on in the rest of the Church. There are a number of trends that need to be identified, and several new resources and approaches that give grounds for considerable hope.

Finding the best starting point

The first point to note, probably so simple that it can be overlooked, is that any church that does its job well, whatever its form or tradition, will be far more likely to grow. Natural Church Development (NCD),[2] and the slightly lighter Healthy Churches[3] materials, provide significant insights into how this can be done in a targeted way. If the prospect of improving everything all at once is too much for any congregation to face, the NCD approach of identifying one key area for each local church to start with is strongly recommended. Within the Church of England, the Diocese of Coventry has been working for some time with NCD as the focus of its mission strategy, encouraging every congregation to examine its health and to focus on the aspects most in need of enhancement. It is too early to assess the impact of this venture as we write, but it may provide a significant pointer to the potential of NCD as a central and coordinated strategy across a significant geographical area of the Church.

The growth of cathedrals, and other high-profile churches able to match them in terms of style, is now well attested. Bob Jackson identifies the quality of worship – interestingly, generally not in its most traditional form – as being one key reason for growing cathedral congregations.[4] Added to this is the range of services available in most cathedrals, on weekdays as well as Sundays. Put most simply, if there are more services, more people will come. This may not be a realistic aim for some local churches, but often the introduction of an extra midweek service, be it more liturgical than Sunday worship or very informal, will reach some who would probably not be present on a Sunday. If the fresh expressions movement has broken out of the mould of Sunday-morning-only worship, it is often a simple step for traditional churches to follow suit.

Baptisms, weddings and funerals: absorbing time and energy?

In traditional churches, contact with the surrounding population at, or close to, life's great landmarks – birth, marriage and death – has been a priority for generations. This is especially true within the Church of England, claiming, as it does, that through the parish system it reaches all who live in an area, and not only those who are regular churchgoers. It is also an accepted truth that the multiple pastoral contacts provided through baptisms, weddings and funerals are fruitful soil, within which deeper faith and full church allegiance can be enabled to grow.

Surprisingly to many, Bob Jackson's careful research in the Diocese of London would appear to indicate a sharply different reality, within the capital at least.[5] Smaller numbers of baptisms, weddings and funerals – known together as 'occasional offices' – correlate strongly with higher church attendance. When setting his figures alongside the wider loss of a sense of Christendom in the fast-changing culture of Britain's biggest urban centre, Jackson concludes: 'these two factors are connected the opposite way round from the traditional theory that the church is built by the pastoral contacts of the occasional offices, for they are enormously time consuming.'[6]

In other words, the extra time taken up by more occasional offices in other parts of the country, amounting, Jackson calculates, to between half and one whole day per week, is time not spent doing other things. In settings where very few occasional offices are now requested, the most effective first response may well not be to seek to encourage more of them. A better use of limited time may be directed towards some of the other things we consider within this book, for example enquirers' courses, Messy Church or community action in partnership with others. Through these, requests for baptism, weddings and funerals are likely to follow, but the relationships upon which those requests are based will be stronger, and set in a context where further deepening may become a natural process.

However, the capital is not the whole country. One minister who had moved from London to Sheffield made the following significant observation:

> From my experience of ministry in London, occasional offices frequently can get in the way. This is because the population are often highly transient. The chances of next of kin, baptism families or married couples still living nearby even a few months after a service are limited. Outside of London where population is more stable you have a much greater chance of follow-up visits and deeper connections. I will get stopped in the street and thanked for a funeral I did months ago. That never happened in London.

Occasional offices remain highly significant in the majority of churches and in the minds of the people around them. Seeking actively to reduce numbers will serve only to harm the relationship between Church and community. A negative response will simply give the impression of a Church that wants to slam the doors at the very moment when people may most feel the need to seek after God.

Baptisms, weddings and funerals: taking the opportunities

Research carried out for the Church of England's Weddings Project, and recent follow-up work on the response of families to church contact through baptism, reveals remarkably high levels of satisfaction in people's experience with their local church. The great majority of wedding couples found the involvement with church either positive or very positive, and of couples seeking baptism for their child, 77 per cent of parents wanted to keep in touch with the church.[7] But the fading of Christendom may mean that it is no longer the default option to seek out the Church at life's landmarks. This can be especially marked in urban areas; as one vicar commented, 'I'm in an inner-urban very diverse Birmingham parish. Weddings? Last one was over two years ago. Baptisms? Two kids and two adults this year! Funerals? A few, perhaps 12 a year.'

As a result, those who do make contact with the Church, when this is no longer the 'obvious' thing to do, are likely to have a significantly more serious intention than might have been the case in the past. A trend towards slightly later baptisms, with toddlers being presented more frequently than newborn babies, also puts questions of parenting, communicating faith, and praying with children more directly on the agenda and immediately opens the door to deeper conversation.

The Weddings Project research pointed out another, important reality. People looking for a church wedding valued highly the personal contact with a Christian minister – invariably referred to as 'the Vicar' – to welcome and to guide them through the whole process. This is very encouraging, since it indicates that much of what the clergy do is greatly appreciated. On the other hand, it points up the challenge faced in weaving occasional offices into the worshipping life of the wider church.

Unsurprisingly, clergy tend to have strong views, and have expressed them to us in the process of writing. Some spoke powerfully of the potential they saw in these points of contact. One wrote: 'I get the equivalent of two-thirds of the entire parishes' populations through the door of the church in any one year and an opportunity to both show the love of God in Jesus Christ and to speak of it.' However, the same respondent went on to comment: 'The follow-on, however, in terms of at least overt expressions of faith, is very slim.'

Others were rightly keen to point out that this is more than the simple link between one contact and one local church. It is part of the Church's wider engagement with society. One commented:

From my own vicaring experience, occasional offices are fundamental to incarnational ministry. My own church may not feel the immediate benefit in terms of bums on seats on a Sunday morning, but often people's experience of church at major turning points in life will colour their perception of church for the rest of their lives, which means that 20 years down the line, people may feel able to cross the threshold when they wouldn't have done before.

This was borne out by the positive observation of a Roman Catholic woman: 'I hear wonderful things from non-churchgoers week in and out about the welcome they received at baptisms and funerals.'

Baptisms, weddings and funerals: welcome and community

Some ministers in large parishes report numbers that make realistic follow-up all but impossible. The demographic profile may mean that a focus of energy on just one of the services is the best starting point. In middle-class areas where marriage is still the norm, or in places where a pretty church makes an attractive venue, weddings may be the best focus of energy. Where the surrounding population is elderly, funeral ministry will be a natural priority. That is not to say, of course, that other pastoral contacts should not be approached in a warm and caring way, but it may be that one area can naturally be prioritized for a fully developed strategy. The Church of England's excellent weddings preparation website (<www.yourchurchwedding.org>) has now been joined by extensive new resources for christenings (a term used deliberately to reflect the language most current with families making an initial approach) and funerals (<https://churchsupporthub.org>).

In the case of funerals, with advance warning naturally being limited, the main focus will be sensitive, caring guidance for those in shock. For weddings and baptisms, preparation time is available. The key element of this seems to be a focus on *welcome*, not triage. Many approach the Church with trepidation, and if they are given the message that their enquiry is received with delight the process from then onwards can be positive for all parties. While offering the chance to join a discipleship course may be warmly accepted, it can actually cut across the very intention of such a course if it is seen as a mandatory requirement, perhaps one necessary for a child's baptism to go ahead. As the introduction to Alpha at Holy Trinity Brompton puts it: 'You don't have to come for the whole term – just pop along for the first session and see what you think. No pressure, no follow up and no charge.' The integrity of Alpha or its equivalents can be compromised if it is seen as a hoop to jump through before an occasional office can be accessed.

If possible, a key step is moving on from encounter with a welcoming *person* to discovering a welcoming *community*. Research for the Christenings Project indicates 29 per cent of people who had their child baptized in the context of Sunday worship becoming regular churchgoers, compared with 14 per cent where the ceremony took place outside the main service. Of course, this may say something about the nature of Sunday services, and whether or not they are capable of welcoming a christening party in a positive way; but if Sunday worship is not able to welcome children and families, the next challenge in enabling growth may well be to address just that.

Sunday worship may not be the best place for people to continue a journey of exploring faith and growing in belonging, however, and different ways in may be suggested. One archdeacon, looking back on the place of funerals in bringing people to faith, commented:

> Tuesday Fellowship met in the afternoon every week and it was easy to suggest that the recently bereaved could join that group – instead of Sunday church. There they would meet people in a similar situation. If possible we would link them up with an existing member and get them to invite the newly bereaved person. This is easier than it may seem as you can make connections at the funeral service – looking out for those who attend Tuesday Fellowship already and who are at the funeral service.

One priest always completes baptism planning details with the family during coffee after a morning service, so that the initial point of contact is in the midst of a warm and welcoming community. A rehearsal for the baptism service is then conducted by lay people, broadening the range of faces that would be familiar to the family, and deepening involvement with the Christian community.

Continuing the journey

Once occasional offices are seen as positive points of contact at significant life moments, the way forward is to help people

144

continue the journey from that point onwards. We are, in essence, suggesting a shift in emphasis from preparation to follow-on. One excellent resource, Ally Barrett's *Making the Most of Your Child's Baptism*,[8] is full of useful ideas on praying and exploring faith as a family as children grow. Especially true in the case of infant baptisms, taking the opportunity to encourage people to carry on the journey from a point of openness is true for funerals too.

> Having been taking funerals for over 30 years, I find that I am becoming bolder in trying to give content to the Christian hope, and as a result have noticed more people joining the church following the funeral of a loved one. I now include the tribute at the start of the funeral service – often given by a family member or friend – so that after the Bible reading I can speak about Jesus and the resurrection. Then at the end of the service in the crematorium I close with a simple invitation along the lines, 'It may be that being here today has raised important questions in your mind about life and death and what Christians believe about life after death. If so, I have a few booklets here that may just be helpful to you in thinking further about this; if you would like one, please ask.' The first time I plucked up courage to do it, I thought to myself, this will seem crass, no one will respond; but in fact three people asked me for a booklet as I shook their hands at the door, and at almost every crematorium service since, someone has requested one.[9] Interestingly, this approach doesn't work nearly as well when conducting a funeral service in church. Perhaps the crematorium is a more anonymous or 'safer' place where it doesn't feel as if there might be strings attached.

Some parishes use invitation cards, personally signed by the vicar, to invite family members after a funeral to services when they and their loved one will be remembered by name in prayer. Anniversary cards, literature relevant to the culture and setting, as well as personal visiting, can all play their part, and the Soul Food initiative[10] of the Dioceses of Birmingham and St Albans allows people to sign up for text messages or emails over the following weeks that can keep interest and exploration alive.

Even when there is no immediate pattern of church attendance as a result of these points of contact, the positive impact should not be underestimated. Families will often appreciate being kept in touch, maintaining the sense that they belong, even while at the same time football, shopping and other sources of competition may work against regular attendance at worship. The next point may well be at another of life's landmarks: another christening as a second child is born; christenings increasingly lead to weddings; weddings are followed by more baptism contact; or the funeral of one partner leads to further sad but already familiar family contact when the surviving partner also dies. The key is to remember the ongoing attachment of the whole family to 'their' church, even though they may still be some way from regular Sunday worship.

A growing number of churches are making imaginative use of annual special events, giving opportunities to revisit and to mark afresh the step taken at a baptism, wedding or funeral. Services 'In Loving Memory' can provide an annual marker at which loved ones are remembered once again, candles lit, flowers distributed and prayers said. Another parish has an annual Valentine's theme for a creative evening service in February, to which couples can be invited to celebrate their wedding in the church. One village has an annual Summer Celebration of Baptism to which all who have been baptized, of any age, are invited, with Pimm's and soft drinks on the lawn afterwards. Occasional offices can weave in with the landmarks of the year shared by everyone, and it is to those we turn next.

Seasons and festivals, old and new

While the number of people seeking out a church for baptisms, wedding and funerals may be in decline, the totals are still significant, as we have seen. But it is not only the seasons of life that are marked in many traditional churches. The seasons of the year and the annual rhythm are of great importance, often but not always in the countryside. Christmas, or more specifically the lead-up to Christmas and in particular carol services, continues to provide contact with millions each year. Easter may barely show as a blip on the attendance graph in urban areas, and certainly the message is more challenging to handle than what is encountered at most Christmas services, but in other places Easter Day will see traditional churches packed with people who may have had little contact since the Christmas midnight service.

The pattern across the country is mixed. Traditional festivals would appear to be having far less impact in urban areas. Some festivals are on the way to disappearing, with Mothering Sunday and Harvest Festival struggling to survive in some settings. Mothering Sunday, in particular, is rapidly completing its transition to Mother's Day, increasingly privatized and a time for taking Mum or Grandma out to lunch rather than going to church. On the other hand, the profile of Remembrance Sunday has been raised recently with military involvement overseas, and many churches report growing attendance at what appeared 20 years ago to be another fading festival. The impact of secularization is not uniform, and the para-Christian festivals of the year – as distinct from specifically Christian celebrations such as Easter, Pentecost and Christmas – can still have significant impact if there remains a felt need in wider society to mark them.

There is no theological imperative for churches to celebrate festivals that are not specifically Christian in nature; on the other hand, some festivals marking the high points of the Church's year have been unknown for years to the bulk of the population. Pentecost and Trinity Sunday, for example, carry no particular expectation that crowds of local people will join in, and remembering the key elements of the Christian story is largely about discipling those who are already worshippers. On the other hand, there is no special reason to keep Harvest Festival – a brilliant new idea of Parson Hawker in Morwenstow back in 1843 – if it fails now to speak to the community. What traditional churches can do, like Parson Hawker in his day, is to create new traditions.

One highly effective new tradition is Christingle, brought from Moravia by the Church of England Children's Society in 1968 and now an annual fixture in many places. It resonates with a broad desire to mark the power of light over darkness, and feels

Christmassy in a general way, but can be used flexibly across the season and need not clash with family, school or other Christmas events.

There is more that can and should be done in thinking how seasons, annual landmarks and life stages can be marked in fresh ways in old settings. This will mean weaving together an attachment to church buildings as places where many in the community gather at significant moments with informed and attentive understanding of what those significant moments now are, and what feelings people need help in exploring. If there is not a church marking Red Nose Day with creative worship and fun, there really ought to be! One of the starting points of the Fresh Expressions movement is listening to the community. Traditional churches need to listen too, and the potential for new traditions to emerge from that listening is considerable.

May Day in Toft

In Toft, a village of 500 people a few miles from Cambridge, one of the seasonal highlights is the Sunday before May Day. Beginning back in the early 1990s, and emerging from shared plans of some who were church members and some who were not, it now forms part of a whole weekend 'Feast' of celebration and shared activity. The Sunday involves a village boundary walk, Maypole dancing, well blessing and open-air tea on the lawn of the manor house. Worship takes place in both the Methodist and Anglican churches, with the local folk band providing music, and people packing the church building in the afternoon in a way that has not been seen for years at other festivals. May Day is now a fixture, and one of the new seasonal points when the church is making contact with a very significant proportion of the village's population.

Back to Church Sunday

One national initiative that has the potential to establish a new festival is Back to Church Sunday.[11] Bringing together national publicity with adaptable resources for invitation and worship, Back to Church Sunday has the potential to be an annual landmark, a repeatable opportunity for recommitment on the part of those who have slipped out of church attendance. The stated aim is not to reach out to the completely unchurched, but to let those who feel uneasy about returning know that there is a warm welcome. Significantly, it implies that those who come back will not be the only ones, since the fear of being spotted and exposed can hold people back from re-engaging with church.

At the time of writing the continued impact of Back to Church Sunday is not entirely clear. Some churches report moderate success in terms of small numbers of people coming to a special service and continuing as church members. In rural areas particularly the timing can clash with Harvest Festival, but that can itself still have a definite 'back to church' intention where it continues to flourish. In recognition of this, the Back to Church originators have moved to an extended emphasis, linking together autumn and early winter events into a Season of Invitation.

Back to Church Sunday has not succeeded in establishing a clear national presence, and it has the disadvantage of being a church-based initiative rather than a response to felt needs in society more widely. It is interesting to note how Christingle has met a felt need, is sought out by many in the wider community enquiring about seasonal services, and may currently be a better point of invitation. If All Souls' services are added to this, and Remembrance Sunday maintains its current high profile, the later months of the year will hold a range of events, each having their own level of significance in each local area, that can be used to create an extended period of engagement and invitation, leading up to the annual high point of Christmas. Invitation is not in itself, of course, a way to discipleship, but it is a beginning. John's Gospel starts with the repeated request, first by Jesus and then by his friends, to 'Come and see', and from that a journey of discipleship began. Traditional churches still have many moments of invitation. If those who accept the offer do indeed see something of Jesus when they attend, a journey as disciples may be about to begin.

Everybody Welcome

Occasional visitors to traditional churches, whether to seasonal services or at weekly worship, may or may not return. Often the key factor in deciding the next step is the quality of welcome. While this is not always the case (in smaller churches the welcome may be so enthusiastic that enquirers have little opportunity to sit in the back row and think without being engaged in hearty conversation), in settings where the congregation is over 100 strong, for example, deliberate attention to the quality of welcome will be essential if visitors are not to walk away feeling unnoticed. A congregation with the commitment to work hard at this will benefit considerably from the Everybody Welcome course,[12] which addresses not only initial welcome but how this can go on to enable people to feel fully part of the life of the church and to grow as disciples.

A pattern of mutual support

Churches in inherited mode that continue to flourish will be vital for the ongoing expansion of fresh expressions. Being financially hard-headed about it, Christians who have been church members for a very long time are likely to have disciplines of giving that will provide much of the funding needed for fresh expressions to grow.

Where fresh expressions are already having a major and, we believe, underreported impact is in changing attitudes to mission on the part of other churches. The carefully sifted statistics gathered by the Church Army Research Unit rightly do not count all mission ventures and new initiatives as fresh expressions of church. Approximately half do not 'make the cut', and have been excluded in surveys to date. Some are events that take place less than once a month. Others have no intention of becoming self-supporting churches in their own right. But the point is this – those new ventures are still going on.

Some of the spirit of fresh expressions is pervading much of the Church. There is a growing grasp of the reality that those contacted will never sit on a pew on a Sunday morning. For them, church will always be something else, a different group, a different time. This has been true for many years in youth work, as flourishing groups of young people, supported by individual congregations or groups of churches, lead to young adults living out their discipleship at school, at university or college, and later in working life. Most youth groups may not be defined as fresh expressions of church, but increased understanding of the place of fresh expressions within the whole Church of God may well enable congregations to rejoice at what is going on in the lives of young people through the work of youth ministry locally, and not simply to complain that 'we never see them in church'.

It is likely, then, that a significant number of people are encountering the Christian message and meeting with God, but are recorded neither as members of fresh expressions nor as attending 'standard' churches. Added to this, they may view their involvement with a group or activity that does not take place on a Sunday morning as their main expression of Christian discipleship. In some of our own churches, several regular worshippers will choose to attend a monthly theology group in place of joining Sunday worship. The recorded attendance at church on that week will be lower, but the impact in terms of Christian discipleship may well be far more significant. Thus, the amount of mission work that slips under the radar of churches' statistical analysis is likely to be growing. The Fresh Expressions movement is posing the question, 'Is this a church?' When the answer is 'not quite', God is still very definitely at work.

In Wellington we have noticed a definite trend in recent years of larger and larger numbers attending the civic act of remembrance at the war memorial in the corner of the churchyard (the numbers have more than doubled to around 1,500) while at the same time the numbers attending the parade who then come into church for the shortened morning service immediately afterwards has dropped. Having tried for a few years to invite more people to come into church after the wreath-laying, last year we decided to focus instead on making the act of remembrance outside more complete as an act of worship, with a short story of faith from the trenches and brief thought after the reading. We offered facsimile copies of the 'service issue' Gospel (produced by Scripture Gift Mission) for any who would like to take one as a souvenir, and read for themselves the words that gave strength to many during the First World War.

In pushing the boundaries of our understanding, fresh expressions can also plant ideas that inspire traditional churches. A significant proportion of fresh expressions are led by lay people who have no formal status or recognition within their denominations. As their roles become more widely recognized, and at the same time space becomes available in churches where mission teams have left specifically to set up separate fresh expressions, so the idea of ordinary Christians exercising their leadership gifts within churches could catch on. Indeed, it is usually far easier to lead set liturgy than to start from nothing, and most congregations will contain people who wonder whether they might be able to contribute more, but have held back. The departure of more confident leaders can both inspire and leave space for action. The impact of the 'I could do something too' response as more stories of new church life are told could be quite remarkable.

Once the principle is grasped that fresh expressions are not going to be feeding people into normal Sunday morning church, the way is open for a changed vision of just what the Church is about. By backing up, praying for and being inspired by fresh expressions, members of more traditional congregations can have their vision of God enhanced by observing what is going on. The rhetoric of constant decline is seen to be false, and hope can become something that spreads.

More significantly, fresh expressions and inherited mode churches together, listening to one another and working to see what God is doing, have the potential to grasp a new understanding of the Church of God. It is less a case of 'traditional' and 'fresh' running in parallel but separate from each other, and more one of a changing, emerging shape, with both old and new being changed by mutual understanding, respect, listening and care. The future could be a new shape of church for all of us.

11

Good news: the hidden growth of the common good

———◆·◉·◆———

> Direct this nation and all nations in the ways of justice
> and of peace; that men may honour one another and seek
> the common good.
>
> (Series 2 Order for Holy Communion, 1967)

This chapter has something to celebrate, regarding the way that different theological traditions have come to affirm the place of both social action *and* evangelism in the mission of the Church. The paradox for those passionate about evangelism used to be, 'Can we afford to spend time on social action, when we urgently need to save souls?', while those passionate about social action used to ask in return, 'Why are you worried about bums on seats when what really matters is the kingdom of God?' Now, there is increasing agreement across the traditions that both are vital, and that social action helps Christians to grow as disciples of Jesus, and gives evangelism its integrity.

The good news about the common good is partly that evangelicals have rediscovered their social conscience, which they mislaid in the early twentieth century, in reaction against the Social Gospel movement. It is also that socially active liberals have rediscovered their theology, and in particular the biblical foundations for social engagement. As Malcolm Brown has argued, the *Faith in the City* report (1985), which was so strong and influential in its analysis of the plight of the inner cities, was weak in its theology, relying too much on South American liberation theology rather than on the more culturally relevant work of William Temple earlier in the twentieth century.[1] There is now a resurgence of interest in developing a truly Anglican social theology, inspired by the longer tradition of Catholic Social Teaching, building on the foundations laid in William Temple's *Christianity and Social Order*[2] and engaging with the growing evangelical scholarship on the biblical foundations for social action.[3]

The 'common good'

The idea that Christians are called to 'honour one another and seek the common good' has embedded itself in the mind of Anglican worshippers through constant repetition in intercessory prayer at the Eucharist over the past 40 years, since it was introduced in the old Series 2. Following immediately after petitions for the Queen and all in authority, these words have helped to form the idea in generations of churchgoers that pursuing the common good is a priority not only for personal discipleship but also for political leaders. As the House of Bishops commented in their pastoral letter for the 2015 General Election:

> The privileges of living in a democracy mean that we should use our votes thoughtfully, prayerfully, and with the good of others in mind, not just our own interests. Pursuing the common good is a Christian obligation and is expressed in how we approach our role as voters as much as in our personal priorities.[4]

However, the idea of the common good goes a lot further back than the 1960s. It is first expressed as a philosophical idea in Aristotle's *Politics*,[5] which influenced Christian thought through Aquinas and Ignatius. The phrase also appears in the *Epistle of Barnabas*, and is strongly present in Augustine of Hippo's *City of God*. In Book XIX Augustine addresses the question of whether human well-being is found in the good of the whole society (the common good) to which he answers a very clear 'yes'. Aquinas asserts that the common good is discovered not just in political structures but in the ties of affection that bind people together in families and communities.

Aquinas' teaching on the common good has become enshrined in Catholic Social Teaching. *The Common Good* is the title of an important document from the Roman Catholic Bishops' Conference of England and Wales, published in 1996. This paper established the importance within Catholic Social Teaching of the pursuit of the common good as an obligation on both Church and state. It provoked an exceptionally positive response across the Christian churches of Britain. The 2004 *Compendium of the Social Doctrine of the Church*, quoting the Vatican II document *Gaudium et spes*, says, 'According to its primary and broadly accepted sense, *the common good* indicates "the sum total of social conditions which allow people, either as groups or as individuals, to reach their fulfilment more fully and more easily".'[6] The Compendium itself goes further still, suggesting that the common good describes not only the social conditions that enable people to reach fulfilment, but also the goal of human life itself: 'The goal of life in society is in fact the historically attainable common good.'[7]

An idea whose time has come

It is remarkable how the language of the common good has gained traction across the churches in recent years. 'Promoting the common good' became one of the three Quinquennial Goals adopted by the Church of England in 2010, along with 'promoting numerical and spiritual growth' and 'reimagining ministry'. A clue as to how this particular goal has caught the imagination of the church can be found by searching the Church of England website – there are 59 results for the words 'reimagining ministry', 560 results for 'evangelism' and 1,800 results for 'common good'.[8] It is fair to say that the idea of the common good has captured the imagination in the churches in a way that the somewhat related idea of the 'Big Society' never did in the nation as a whole.

As the Church of England's 2010 strategy document put it:

Anglican theology, like Catholic Social Teaching, grounds the importance of the common good upon the intrinsic dignity of every human being. All bear God's image and all are loved by the God who desires their flourishing . . . It is not just a matter of empirical fact, but an aspect of the created order, that human beings flourish best in social relationships – starting with the family but extending much further in the wider 'families' of community, church and nation as well as in global affinities within the human family itself.[9]

The massive and growing involvement of Christians, partnering with those outside the churches, in work for justice and mercy in society is one of the most heartening signs of the health of the Christian Church. It has been calculated that church members (of all denominations) in England give more than 23 million hours of volunteer time every month outside of the regular work of the Church.[10] Although overall attendance figures may be falling, attendance at public worship is only one way to measure a church. While attendance is a measure of the *breadth* of the church, two other dimensions are equally important: the *depth* of faith of its members and the *vitality* of the church, as evidenced by the ministry and service offered by its members, in the workplace and the community, as an instrument, sign and foretaste of the kingdom of God. A holistic vision for the growth of the church is one that seeks growth in all three dimensions, in numbers, spirituality and effectiveness.

The common good and evangelism

The pursuit of the common good provides an important counterbalance at a time when most denominations are taking steps to address long-term numerical decline. A church that was simply pursuing numerical and spiritual growth could quickly be perceived as being turned in on itself, engaged in mission for the sake of the Church rather than for the sake of the world. Ann Morisy comments, 'Anxiety turns us inwards and drains us of energy, so we get preoccupied with more and more analysis and dare only to tweak the structures, rather than turn outwards to practise Gospel obedience in our neighbourhoods and world.'[11] Or, as Pope Francis has put it:

> We need to avoid the spiritual sickness of a Church that is wrapped up in its own world: when a church becomes like

this it grows sick. It is true that going out onto the street implies the risk of accidents happening, as they would to any ordinary man or woman. But . . . if I had to choose between a wounded Church that goes out onto the streets and a sick withdrawn Church, I would definitely choose the first one.[12]

By contrast, a church that is focused outwards, on the common good of all, is offering something very attractive to those who have grown weary of the individualism and materialism of so much of contemporary culture. In a world in danger of becoming 'a society of strangers' (to quote a phrase from the House of Bishops' pastoral letter), offering a vision of a society that is 'a community of communities' is part of the gospel the Church offers to the world – a vision of living well.[13]

We would suggest that the language of the common good has offered churches a way to move beyond the rather tired dichotomy between social action and evangelism. As recent ecumenical agreements have affirmed, the Church is called into being by God not for its own sake but to be a sign, instrument and foretaste – that is, a sacrament – of the kingdom of God.[14] Increasingly churches that have been strong on evangelism but weak on social action are realizing that if people are to receive life in all its fullness (John 10.10) they need help to escape the grip of deprivation, debt and despair – witness the massive growth of evangelically based organizations like Christians Against Poverty (discussed below).

Likewise, there are signs that churches that have been strong on social action but weak on evangelism are realizing that unless the church is consistently making new disciples then its ability to be a force for good in society will decline, as its membership grows smaller and more elderly. As the Church of England's report on the common good stated:

Any tendency to see the pursuit of the common good as a discrete activity somehow detached from the worshipping and missionary life of the church is mistaken. Building up the church is part of the Christian commitment to the common good since the good cannot be fully realised apart from Christ, and Christ cannot be fully known outside the community of the faithful. William Temple makes this point very clearly at the end of his seminal *Christianity and Social Order*. 'If we have to choose between making men Christian and making the social order more Christian, we must choose the former. But there is no such antithesis. Certainly there can be no Christian society unless there is a large body of convinced and devoted Christian people to establish it and keep it true to its own principles.'[15]

The 'Isaiah vision' revisited

We detect signs that the ideas of Raymond Fung have filtered through into the mainstream: seeking the common good need not be an alternative to evangelism (for those who prefer that kind of thing), and can itself be deeply evangelistic. In 1992 Raymond Fung, then secretary for evangelism for the World Council of Churches, published 'an ecumenical strategy for congregation-based evangelism' based on the vision in Isaiah 65.20–23 of a society in which children do not die, old people live in dignity, those who build houses live in them and those who plant vineyards eat their fruit.[16] Fung encouraged local churches to reach out to their neighbours who share that vision for society and to work with them. Along the way, Fung suggested that there would be times when the task would seem too great, when it was natural for Christians to pause and pray, and to invite their neighbours to join them in those moments. As trust and friendships developed, there would then be times when it was appropriate to invite those partnering with the churches to consider the invitation to become disciples of Jesus themselves.

Those *kairos* moments, when those with whom one shares in social action are suddenly open to the possibility of God, and begin to sense that God might be alongside them in their struggles, are explored by Ann Morisy in what she describes as 'apt liturgy'.[17] Apt liturgy may not necessarily be worship as such, but consists of the naming of moments, the articulating of struggles, and relating these to the God who struggles with us to bring about his kingdom of justice and righteousness. The challenge for Christians is to be alert to spot these moments when they arise, and to be 'out and proud' and ready to give a reason for the hope that is within them, but with gentleness and respect (1 Peter 3.15).

Social action 'evangelizes' the faithful

One exciting aspect of the deepening interrelationship between evangelism and the common good is the impact of developing a long-term social action ministry on the members of the local church, as Ann Morisy has highlighted. A recent consultation among diocesan social responsibility officers pointed out the fact that setting up foodbanks in response to local need has become a key part of the discipleship journey of many middle-class churches. By engaging personally with the poor, church members have found that their own comfortable assumptions have been challenged, their appreciation of the biblical 'bias to the poor' has grown, and they have found themselves learning spiritual lessons from those they have sought to help.

Another interesting example of this dynamic is the Besom project, which began when its founder, James Odgers, a successful businessman, visited Hong Kong in 1987. He was introduced by Jackie Pullinger to some of the poorest residents of the Kowloon Walled City, and his life was so transformed by the experience that when he came back he set up Besom at Holy Trinity Brompton, situated in affluent Knightsbridge. The remarkable feature of Besom is that it sees itself as a service to the rich rather than to the poor, helping the 'haves' to grow as disciples by giving them ways to share with those who have not. It provides a bridge between those who want to give and those who are in need, through which a passion for Jesus matures into compassion for those in need. As one of the time-givers quoted on the Besom website says, 'We went as a group thinking we would give a day to paint someone's home and hopefully help them ... but we had no idea that we would come away having gained far more than we gave. Their walls were transformed and so were we.' The Besom model has been replicated in scores of churches across the country and seeks to transform the lives of people who have resources they are willing to give (money, time, skills, or things) by bringing them into direct contact with the lives of people they help.[18]

Building relationships and sharing the experience of those who are poor can have a life-changing impact. Chris Neilson – now Church and Community Officer in the diocese of St Albans – tells how his friendship with a homeless alcoholic changed him.

Jeff had a criminal record listing 217 offences, and 'that's just what they caught me for', he told me. He was my friend. He had been an alcoholic since he was a teenager and has been homeless many times, for many reasons – once was when he got in an argument with the housing office, and jumped over the desk with a machete.

He did a sponsored walk to Blackpool last year, then rang me at 1 a.m. to pick him up; he raised £1,000 that day. Then one of the other homeless guys stole £10 from the pot. Jeff 'lovingly' stamped on his head and left him for dead. The guy staggered to a five-day stay in hospital.

He called all the homeless in Oldham 'scumbags' and 'street rats', yet he went out in the early hours of the morning giving them food and supplies. He has made arrangements to get the left-over food from supermarkets, McDonald's and Greggs bakery, before they throw it away. He'd go round McDonald's collecting stickers for free coffees. He would do this, 'on behalf of the Salvation Army', for which he had no permission or authority.

He was a manipulative bully, who used fear and violence to get what he wanted. He would fight for the weak and abused on the streets of Oldham. He told me he had demons; I told him God loved him.

I learned something about rainbows. When you take visible light and put it through a raindrop (it acts as a prism), it breaks this clear light into its many parts. A rainbow is broken light. Jeff was broken, a very broken person. Scarred by the world and his own decisions, he had done lots of very nasty things, abusing others and himself, yet he did far more for more homeless people in Oldham than I and many others, paid to do so, ever have. Why do I get the credit and he the scorn?

God has shone a beautiful, vibrant light through Jeff's brokenness, and the more I look the more I see his beauty. Some people see others as beyond redemption and forgiveness, thinking that grace is weakness and lacks justice. I praise God for a greater understanding of brokenness and beauty – a God who declares 'good news to the poor', the oppressed, the marginalized and the broken. He turns their weakness into strength, uses the foolish to shame the wise, creates a kingdom where the first shall be last and the last will be first. It's called grace, and it's the measure I want to be judged by. I want the light of God's grace to shine through my brokenness and reflect his beauty.

Last week, I took Jeff's funeral. I had met Jeff when he was living in a tent, pitched in a graveyard. I laid him to rest in that graveyard. What a huge privilege. Thank you, God.

Recent initiatives for the common good

Lots of examples could be cited of the ways in which churches have caught the vision to be engaged with projects that seek the common good in their locality. The following are a few.

Street Pastors

Street Pastors was pioneered in London in 2003 by Pastor Les Isaac. On that first night, 18 volunteers took to the streets of Brixton. Since then they have trained over 12,000 street pastors, active in more than 270 towns and cities around the UK. Street pastors are volunteers from local churches who care about their community. They patrol in teams of men and women, usually from 10 p.m. to 4 a.m. on a Friday and Saturday night, to care for, listen to and help people who are out on the streets. Together with prayer pastors, management teams and trustees, there are over 20,000 volunteers in total associated with the Street Pastors network. There are also a growing number of Street Pastors teams overseas. Each city project is set up by Ascension Trust, the governing body behind Street Pastors, and run by a local coordinator with support from local churches and community groups, in partnership with the police, local council and other statutory agencies.

Street pastors have received a hugely positive press in the secular media, with endorsement from local police chiefs praising them for helping to reduce crime and disorder, and have won many community awards. They are explicitly not there to preach or evangelize, although many volunteers have found themselves involved in fruitful conversations when clients have asked them, 'Why on earth are you here for us at this time of night?'

Foodbanks

Churches have made a massive contribution to the growth and development of foodbanks over recent years. The Trussell Trust was founded by Paddy and Carol Henderson, who were fundraising in Salisbury for their project working with street children in Bulgaria when they received a call from a desperate mother in Salisbury pleading, 'My children are going to bed hungry tonight – what are you going to do about it?' After investigating the needs on their doorstep Paddy started Salisbury foodbank in his garden shed and garage. From that small beginning the Trussell Trust now partners with churches and communities nationwide to open foodbanks. Over 445 have been opened since the network was launched in 2004.

Trussell foodbanks provide a minimum of three days' emergency food and support to people referred to them by churches and other agencies. In 2014–15 they fed over one million recipients nationwide, compared to just 25,000 six years previously. Of those helped, one-third are children. The most common reasons for people being referred to a foodbank are benefit delays, low income and benefit changes – these three factors account for two-thirds of all clients. Other reasons include debt, homelessness and unemployment, and being refused a crisis loan.[19]

'I just think it's outrageous, I'm angry, to be honest with you. No developed country should be in this situation. A lot of people are only one pay cheque away from a disaster.' Cambridge city foodbank helped 4,600 people over the last financial year, up by 80 per cent over the previous 12 months. More than a quarter of these were in work. Every client is referred to the foodbank via a professional agency such as Citizens Advice, doctors or social workers. 'I think the most surprising thing is the need in Cambridge,' says Cathy Michell, who has been volunteering at the foodbank for around a year. 'We provide emergency food to people who are in a genuine emergency and would be going hungry.'[20]

Christians Against Poverty (CAP)

It is estimated that 2.4 million people in Britain have problem debt. Founded by John Kirkby in Bradford in 1996, Christians Against Poverty has grown into a national debt counselling charity with over 270 debt centres.[21] Each centre is sponsored by local Christian churches, and employs one or more debt coaches, who visit clients in their own home and help them develop a plan to get free from debt. Every month 2,000 people ring the free 0800 helpline, and one-third of them are suicidal. CAP is able to help about 12,000 families a year, and on average 12 people become debt-free every single day. Even more impressive, 96 per cent of clients manage to stay out of debt after being helped by CAP. Having developed a good relationship with the industry, CAP has received a number of high-profile awards for the excellence of its service. Besides expanding the number of debt centres to cover greater parts of the country, it also offers CAP money courses (to teach people how to handle money), as well as job clubs and 'release groups' for those with addictions.

However, CAP is not just about debt. It is about Jesus, in a much more explicitly evangelistic way than the other examples in this section. CAP provides not only debt coaches but members of local churches who act as befrienders, walking alongside the clients on the long road to freedom from debt. In the process, many clients come to a Christian faith through the friendship and support of the local church. CAP estimates that over 700 of their clients become Christians every year.

For CAP, social action and evangelism go hand in hand. The founder, John Kirkby, was crippled by unrepayable debt when his business collapsed, and after a seven-year struggle to get free from debt, during which he became a Christian, he set up CAP. Kirkby says that God laid on him 'a heart for the poor to be set free and a heart to see people come to Christ'. Commenting on the befriending scheme, Archbishop Justin Welby, who has become patron of CAP, comments, 'It's really exciting because it means there's a community for those who want it. CAP don't force people into the church or anything like that, but they offer them scope to find the support and love of a Christian community. That's wonderful.'[22]

Credit unions

One of the main causes of people getting trapped in debt is the easy credit and extortionate levels of interest charged by payday loan companies. The financial squeeze of recent years has led to a massive increase in people turning to payday lenders just to get through to the end of the month. According to one survey, a million UK households take out a payday loan each month, at interest rates that can be between 2,000 and 6,000 per cent APR. The danger of getting caught in endless debt is illustrated by the fact that a quarter of all loans are taken out to repay existing payday loans.

Credit unions are a form of not-for-profit social banking, which encourages responsible saving as well as offering affordable loans at manageable rates. However, many people who contact CAP are not able to borrow from a credit union, because most credit unions traditionally require a person to save with them before they can take out a loan. The churches are well placed to raise the profile of credit unions and to enable them to reach out to a wider section of the community. Following high-level talks between the churches, 2015 has seen the launch of the Churches' Mutual Credit Union (CMCU). Initially open to clergy and church workers, who can save through the credit union via payroll giving, the vision is ultimately to open membership to all those who are active members of a local church. By encouraging clergy to join, it is hoped to raise awareness of services credit unions provide – research by the Church Urban Fund showed that only 20 per cent of clergy knew whether a credit union existed in their parish, despite 90 per cent of the population being covered by a local credit union.

Credit unions offer people with regular but modest incomes, like clergy, the ability to smooth out the peaks and troughs, covering single large items (such as a new car) by a combination of saving and borrowing. Attracting people in secure employment into credit unions also has the vital benefit of increasing the asset base and financial security of the union, enabling it to take a more proactive role in social lending to those in need. As the sector expands, existing credit unions are likely to be able to begin offering loans to borrowers who were not previously members. By supporting the credit union movement the churches are able not only to promote the common good locally, but to apply pressure towards a more ethical and just financial system for the country as a whole. The high-profile engagement of the Archbishop of Canterbury with the launch of CMCU has prompted many churches to make contact with their local credit unions and offer support, often in terms of volunteer helpers or office space.

Good news for the church, bad news for society?

When I feed the poor, they call me a saint, but when I ask why the poor are hungry, they call me a communist.
(Dom Hélder Câmara)

The remarkable growth of the commitment of church members over the last 40 years to seeking 'the ways of justice and of peace, that we may honour one another and seek the common good' is perhaps evidence that prayer works! Certainly it is a heartening sign of the strength and vitality of the Church, and its determination to remain outward-looking and kingdom-focused, when it could easily become preoccupied with the problem of a shrinking and ageing membership. The increasing partnership between those whose passion is evangelism and those whose passion is social justice is enabling the churches to present a more holistic gospel to the world, and making its evangelism credible.

However, to look at it another way, can the growth of the Church's engagement with the common good actually be seen as a disturbing sign of the growing inequality and 'disease' of society, as state provision is cut back in so many areas? Much as I am encouraged by the sight of my church members filling a dustbin with non-perishable foods every Sunday morning for our local foodbank, somewhere deep down I am also seething with anger that so many families are going hungry that a foodbank is needed in my leafy market town on the edge of Telford – in what is still the sixth richest nation on earth. Is supporting a local foodbank merely an easy way for members of my congregation to alleviate the symptoms of poverty and make themselves feel better, when what we should really be doing is something much more radical, challenging the injustices in society that have caused them to mushroom? As Jonathan Chaplin comments, evangelicals have a much stronger history of social action than of social theology.[23] Perhaps the collection for the local foodbank is a reminder of the urgent need for all sections of the Church not only to care for the poor but also to develop a social theology that addresses the prevailing structures of society at a systematic level.

On the other hand, when I calm down, I wonder if the foodbank may just be a sign of a return to a more caring, sustainable society, where people look out for one another, where voluntarism is encouraged and where we no longer pass by on the other side, content to leave the needs of the poor to the welfare state. William Beveridge, the great architect of the welfare state, followed his report on social security with another on Voluntary Action, which affirmed the place of individual voluntary action, alongside the role of the state, in combating the 'five giant evils' of want, disease, ignorance, squalor and idleness. Seventy years on from Beveridge, and this side of the financial crash of 2008, perhaps the churches' involvement in promoting the common good is helping to foster the kind of 'Big Society' that is needed in these straitened times, where the voluntary sector has a key role to play in a more sustainable and affordable model of social provision. After all, in answer to Cain's primal question that has echoed down the millennia, 'I *am* my brother's keeper.'

12

Church-shaped disciples, or disciple-shaped Church?

———◆•◆•◆———

> All ministries, therefore, must be subjected to this
> test – if they do not glorify Christ, they are not of
> the Holy Spirit.
>
> (C. H. Spurgeon)

Not converts but disciples

Throughout this book our focus has returned to the centrality
of making disciples. Both the need for making disciples and the
challenge of doing so are significant. Mere converts or interested
attenders are increasingly unlikely to feel satisfied in a church
that finds itself closer to the margins of society: sticking with a
church that is estranged from much of contemporary culture
is a challenge. It will require dedicated followers to make that
commitment. But maybe, too, if discipleship is part of the fabric
of the church's life, those new disciples will be of fundamental
importance in challenging their fellow believers to grapple with
those very issues of disconnect between church culture and
'normal' life.

Across the church spectrum there is widespread recognition that
Christians must be more than simply converts, attenders or even
members. The role of ministry, therefore, is to equip the whole
of God's people, enabling them to play a full part as followers of
Jesus in building his church. A recent document from a major
Pentecostal denomination has expressed it this way:

> ministry is the work of the entire body of Christ, not just
> of a special priestly or clerical caste. Even the ministries of

168

apostle, prophet, evangelist, and pastor-teacher do not exist as ends in themselves or as rewards for a special elite. They are expressly given 'to prepare God's people for works of service (*diakonía*), so that the body of Christ may be built up' (Ephesians 4.12).[1]

The ordinal of the Church of England also recognizes the central enabling role of the clergy in helping the whole Christian community to grow in faith. Ministers are exhorted not only to care, but to foster growth to maturity:

> With the Bishop and their fellow presbyters, they are to sustain the community of the faithful by the ministry of word and sacrament, that we all may grow into the fullness of Christ and be a living sacrifice acceptable to God.[2]

Professor David Voas, commenting on recent research into church growth conducted by the Church of England, has identified the key roles of both wise ministry and shared reflection:

> What seems crucial is that congregations are constantly engaged in reflection; churches cannot soar on autopilot. Growth is a product of good leadership (lay and ordained) working with a willing set of churchgoers in a favourable environment.[3]

Discipleship, when placed at the heart of all Christian ministry, will seek to emphasize this shared task. Although willing churchgoers are no bad thing (and presumably of far more use than reluctant churchgoers), a church of disciples will involve all members being far more than just willing attenders. This points us to a deeper aspect of discipleship that will be explored further below: the role of disciples not only in growing personally, but as decision-makers and direction-setters.

Mike Breen has written extensively on the centrality of discipleship in 'missional communities', mid-sized groups somewhere between the small home group and the whole congregation, with a dynamic of mission woven into them.[4] At the heart of the missional community is a balance of the three dynamics: in, up, out. Members are encouraged to grow closer to one another (in), to develop their relationship with God (up) and to reach out to the world around in love and witness (out). For Breen, effective discipleship builds the Church, not the other way round. 'We need to understand the church as the *effect* of the discipleship and not the *cause*. If you set out to build a church, there is no guarantee you will build disciples.'[5] In other words, while growing disciples and affirming the centrality of discipleship within the Church is a key priority for those already in existing congregations, the significance is greater than even this. In a challenging, post-Christian culture, growing disciples is likely to be the only way the Church itself will grow and flourish. As we said in Chapter 2, the best way to grow the Church is to grow people.

Not clients but partners

Disciples will grow in a culture where discipleship is the norm for all believers. Only those who are themselves disciples will be able to model what that involves. Only those who are fully involved in the challenges of daily struggling to follow Christ, and who make no claim to have completed that journey, will be able with integrity to ask others to follow them. Thus St Paul is able to write without arrogance to the Philippians: 'Keep on doing the things that you have learned and received and heard and seen in me.'[6] Only a few sentences before, Paul has written of knowing and becoming like Christ:

> Not that I have already obtained this or have already reached the goal; but I press on to make it my own, because Christ Jesus has made me his own. Beloved, I do not consider that I have made it my own; but this one thing I do: forgetting what lies behind and straining forward to what lies ahead, I press on towards the goal for the prize of the heavenly call of God in Christ Jesus.[7]

For Paul, the invitation to follow his example is possible because, and only because, that example is one of learning and growing, of still being a work in progress.

170

Any focus on discipleship that sees ministers, and especially ordained ministers, as somehow themselves exempt from the need for further growth, as leaders while others follow, is rightly open to challenge. One commentator, in a highly sceptical response to a recent Church of England report on the centrality of discipleship, wrote:

> Presumably, the reason that the theologically peripheral concept of 'discipleship' is made to do so much work in these reports is that 'following Jesus' is being used as an analogue for leadership (Jesus and clergy), and followership (laity).[8]

The voice of Jesus calling 'Follow me' cannot really be described as 'theologically peripheral', since it provides the foundation of his relationship with his disciples. On the other hand, a concept of discipleship that involves merely following the vicar – or even the bishop – deserves to be not merely peripheral but banished. Vicars and bishops need to be clear that they are followers and learners, along with all the rest of God's people.

As a curate, enthused by the thought of all the Church of England was about to receive as I launched into public ministry, I was soon fascinated by the example of the vicar with whom I was training. Each time we heard a talk, went to a training day or shared in a discussion group, he seemed immediately to take something from the experience and weave it into the way he did things. Services were led just that bit differently, meetings changed shape, even hand gestures sometimes altered. While I was still confident in my own abilities, I was expected to follow someone who very clearly considered himself a learner. After a few months, I recognized that he was right, and that I still had a very great deal to learn – and resolved to start learning.

The idea that all are learners and all are followers is by no means a recent innovation. Historically, abbot-bishops in the early stages of the evangelization of England have been identified as setting an important precedent, being in authority and active in mission, yet also subject to monastic obedience. As bishop, they exercised oversight, but as members of a religious order they were subject to the rule of the order and expected to play their part in community life.[9]

If those in position of authority are to be learners, not theological experts who already know everything there is to know, then the converse will also be true. The work of doing theology is not for an elite, but for the whole people of God. The biggest questions with which professors of theology grapple are easily spotted by most articulate nine-year-olds. Why does an all-powerful, loving God let innocent people suffer? If God can answer some prayers, why doesn't he answer all of them? How can Jesus be human but also God, and also the Son of God at the same time?

Serious, deep theology can be communicated simply by authors who understand how to grapple with deep issues without resorting to obscurantist language.[10] Indeed, sometimes it is tempting to ask whether those who cannot put profound theological ideas into accessible language have fully grasped them themselves! More importantly, the model of the rabbi and his followers, or of St Paul with his missionary companions, is founded upon example and conversation. Theology is lived and talked. A Church committed to making disciples will be one where theology is set loose, not viewed as too difficult, or possibly even too dangerous, for 'ordinary' believers.

Being visible

It is not the proclamation of the good news alone that sets people on the road of following Jesus, but the sight of that good news in action, the witness of authentic lives. Postmodern culture is wary of claims that something may be 'true', but drawn by evidence that it 'works'. Genuine discipleship is an indicator of authenticity.

A commitment to incarnational ministry has been central to the life of the Church of England for centuries. The challenge for contemporary church life is that incarnational presence has historically been very largely associated with the presence of an ordained, stipendiary priest at the heart of the community. Yes, the congregation has had its part to play, but the focus has been on the ordained person as the representative figure. When people look to see what 'the Church' is doing, they have tended to turn their attention to the vicar.

The experience of the dedicated, personal ministry of priests is one of the main reasons why people offer for ordination. People have, for generations, felt called to care and to share the gospel in the context of the community in which they serve. As we saw in Chapter 10, this has often been expressed in the wise and gentle use of opportunities provided by baptisms, weddings and funerals, as well as in the tradition of general pastoral visiting. 'Incarnational' ministry has thus depended overwhelmingly on the presence of the individual ordained minister. However much that minister may have seen his – and only very recently, her – presence as symbolic of the whole Church, the reality was that the individual, personal presence of the recognized person in recognizable dress provided the heart of the Church's incarnational presence.

Although there may be limited clear evidence of a cause and effect, the reality of the last few decades has been that declining church attendance and a reduction in numbers of paid clergy have gone hand in hand. A general sense that 'the vicar doesn't visit any more' can be one part of the wider perception of a shrinking Christian presence in society.

Over the last 20 years the pattern has not, of course, simply been one of fewer clergy. Within the Church of England, the decision to allow the ordination of women to the priesthood in 1992 brought increased numbers of gifted and dedicated stipendiary ministers. It also coincided with, and added significantly to, the growth of non-stipendiary (unpaid) ministry in the Church. Active retired clergy have a very significant impact too, and many rural parishes would cease to function without their involvement. Yet even allowing for these developments, the decline in the number of hours available from the clergy has continued, and despite relatively healthy numbers offering for ordination this fails to match the larger proportion of active clergy reaching retirement age each year.

We remain convinced of the need for a strong core of full-time, paid ministers at the heart of the life of the Church. But this cannot in itself be the basis for a future growth strategy. If Christ's Church is to follow his incarnational example, then the whole Church needs to play a full part in this. Here John Finney's work in *Finding Faith Today* also offers hope.[11] Alongside the major role played by Christian ministers in bringing people to faith, he identifies two other very highly significant influences on people becoming believers: first, Christian family members and second, Christian friends. Relying on clergy to bring people to faith may be less effective than it has been in the past, but the whole body of believers – known, living and articulate disciples – holds the key to mission in the future.

Without distinctive robes or a white collar, the ordinary believer does not have the recognizable and special status of members of the clergy. But nor do ordinary Christians have the baggage of being perceived as out of touch, unlike 'normal' people, that clergy can sometimes carry. Once 'normal' people are found to be believers, the possibility opens up that others might also be normal and yet be believers. They may feel like 'work in progress', but since it is God at work, that is no bad thing. Not only do lay Christians make up the vast majority of the church, their gifts and witness can have an impact on places where clergy cannot so easily expect to go.

The Diocese of Ely has adopted a diocesan vision introduced with the words: 'We pray to be generous and visible people of Jesus Christ.' Many believers show remarkable generosity in caring for neighbours, supporting voluntary organizations or raising money for a range of charities. The problem is that they are generous, but not visible. A deeply engrained British fear of 'blowing your own trumpet' can hold people back from being open about their faith. But here again, self-understanding as disciples is of fundamental significance. There is no arrogance in claiming to be a learner, or in inviting others to join in the process of learning for themselves.

*Is the role to transform society?
Can Church do that?*

A view of ministry that encompasses the whole of the people of God has one major pitfall. Reduced numbers of paid clergy will find it more and more difficult to do all the church stuff that needs doing to keep churches functioning. Yet drawing more people into running the church system can stifle the primary mission to which they are called. 'Shared ministry' that focuses only on ministry in church will work against the more significant sharing in ministry across the whole of life. The discipleship of all God's people, lived out among neighbours, in the workplace, community and politics, is fundamental to the transformation of society. Ministry of all kinds within the Church is there to equip the whole people of God to live and witness in the whole of God's world.

Ministry and recognition

The criteria for identifying future ministers in the Church of England have tended to focus on spotting potential. The most recent document on criteria for ordination training includes: 'F2: Candidates should have potential for exercising leadership'.[12] While there will always be a need to spot potential, fully shared ministry means that significant leadership is already being exercised by lay people, and this is likely to increase. In encouraging people into accredited ministry, lay or ordained, there must be a significant place for *recognition*, for accepting that many people are leaders, pastors or evangelists, and acknowledging the work they are already doing. God is regularly ahead of the system! *or is the system lagging behind God*

As we have seen, research into fresh expressions of church by the Church Army has identified nearly half of fresh expressions being led by 'lay-lay' people.[13] That is to say, they are not only not ordained, they have no formally recognized training or accreditation of any kind. And yet these people are already exercising significant leadership in the growing part of the Church's *the faster God collure moves* life. A majority of them are women. While it may well be that the experience and training people have gained in para-church

behind the farther the Church

175

organizations and new church networks is under-recorded in these figures,[14] it remains the case that much of God's work is being led by those who are currently outside recognized structures of leadership. The urgent task is to catch up with where God is already at work, and to bring appropriate recognition and affirmation without cramping the style of those already moving mission forward.

Mike Moynagh helpfully identifies qualities to be considered in appointing leaders in fresh expressions of church. People need to be:

- grounded spiritually
- gatherers of people
- gifted in drawing out others
- a good fit for their culture.[15]

This is, significantly, not a list of potential qualities, or of qualities that may be developed after training, but those already being evidenced. In other words, far from spotting elements of openness in character and willingness to learn, Moynagh is recognizing how, in the context of fresh expressions of church, those brought into leadership should *already* be not only using but sharing and encouraging the exercise of gifts in ministry. If the whole Church is to breathe in some of that freshness, the potential for and possible evidence of gathering and drawing out others in ministry may well need to be part of what is looked for in all accredited ministry across the Church.

Ministry and freedom

One remarkable aspect of St Paul's ministry as recorded in the book of Acts and in his epistles is the speed with which he appoints elders and then moves on in a number of towns. Remarkably, the churches survive and grow, even though they often contain multiple problems. Similarly, Jesus is surrounded by a group of followers who signally fail to grasp what he is striving to communicate on a number of occasions, yet he sends them out unescorted to preach and to heal the sick. The New Testament records risky ministry. It could all go wrong, and in a number of cases, it does.

The risks of significant damage to the reputation of the Church are real, and hesitancy about loosening control is understandable. But the sobering truth is that numerous scandals involving clergy have occurred over many years, even though rigorous selection and training procedures have been in place. Affirming people in the ministries they already exercise can allow more people to flourish without first being sucked too far into church culture. And that surely is more effective than drawing potential ministers deep into church culture as part of the selection and training process, and then encouraging them to leave it in cross-cultural mission.

Freedom in ministry will involve accepting the challenges of mission in a sometimes hostile climate. It will involve freedom to fail, accepting that more than one option may need to be tried before the best route forward is located. It will also mean being happy with a small-scale definition of success. Most of the life and growth recorded in fresh expressions of church across the country is limited and fragile. Growth will often be slow. Ministers should be cautious of models and stories from other cultures where the relation between Church and society is different. Large churches, even those that are very well known and producing significant numbers of people offering for ordained ministry, are unlikely to provide models that can easily be adopted in the majority of situations. Small, fragile and slow are key words for future ministers to absorb; however, large numbers of small, fragile churches growing slowly but genuinely can transform the landscape.

Agile relational ministry

When everyone is growing as disciples together, ministry will involve both leadership and followership, by the same person, at the same time. It takes place in the context of community, in relationship with others. Placing these two realities alongside each other leads to the next element of ministry: willingness to change role in the light of others' gifting. That means that all ministers, but perhaps especially paid ministers, will need to become increasingly agile.

Agility in ministry may involve changing tasks, leadership style or patterns of relationship as others exercise their gifts. An agile minister with an established teaching ministry may need to be ready, for example, to step back into the role of adviser and supervisor if gifts of teaching are clearly emerging in another church member. That same minister may need to step back once again at a future date if the pattern of available gifts alters once again. Vocation understood as 'I am called to be a preacher' may need to be reimagined as 'I am called to serve with these people as one part of the team', with the clear implication that the role in the team cannot be decided only by an individual sense of calling. The passion for preaching must still remain, but it is not always to be exercised, and perhaps sometimes to be grown in others.

This is not to say that clergy must neglect the particular gifts that they have been given and concentrate simply on filling the gaps left by the developing of lay ministries. Clergy are most effective when they are ministering in their areas of passion. The skill of an agile leader lies in exercising one's own gifts while creating space for others to develop theirs. Passion in ministry must involve passion for being part of a team.

Ministry of this kind will be willing to live with ecclesiological messiness, with the question, 'Is this a church?', and be ready to accept the tension of uncertainty if no clear answer is currently available. Agile ministers will be experts in practical ecclesiology, spotting what might be a church in the future, grappling with the question of how a local gathering can more fully be a church. They may also need to work with those facing the other side of this question, with local congregations perhaps needing to recognize that they are no longer a church, no longer viable, and that their best future is to close as new ventures grow elsewhere or in different ways.

Agile ministers will increasingly find that they have an instinct for noticing where God is leading, and joining in heading in that direction. But they will also need humility and the emotional literacy to recognize that they are not the only ones able to see God's patterns. Often others will have a clearer vision, and the task of the minister is to enable the whole church to accept that insight and move forward in the light of it. The minister's place may have to adjust, from charting the course ahead to enabling the inner workings of the church to follow as others take the direction forward.

Within a community of disciples, and in a context where stipendiary clergy are fewer in number, the central place of the ordained leader will change from being the norm to being an exception. As churches become networks of ministry, rather than spiders' webs with the paid minister at the centre, less and less of the life of the church will go through, or even relate directly to, a paid minister. Ordained and other recognized ministers will continue to be a vital part, but only a part, of the whole of God's work of ministry:

> We might say that a leader is someone who assists others in the performance of a collective practice. Such a leader is not necessarily one who himself or herself excels in the practice, though he or she certainly has to be competent in it. Rather, he or she will be good at participating in that practice in such a way as to draw others deeper into it.[16]

In a culture where the Church is widely perceived as irrelevant or imaginative, ground-breaking entrepreneurial leadership will grow in significance. It may not necessarily be the authorized minister who is the entrepreneur. The designation of pioneer ministry in the light of the *Mission-Shaped Church* report provided the most focused response to this on the part of the Church of England:

> A pioneer minister is someone who has the necessary vision and gifts to be a missionary entrepreneur: with the capacity to form and lead fresh expressions and new forms of church appropriate to a particular culture. Pioneer ministers may be ordained or lay (not ordained) and different denominations and streams have ways of training and authorising pioneer ministers.[17]

Some ministers, both paid and unpaid, will themselves be pioneers. But other clergy and licensed ministers will find that their role is to recognize, protect and support those who are the informal, instinctive and unlicensed pioneers around them. The best ministry may well be unseen, setting others free to break out in new and eye-catching ways. People who put their foot in it are usually walking, not sitting in an armchair, and ministry in the past has perhaps been overcautious and wary of the harm such people can do. There is a need for courage in letting people with energy and vision get out and walk into new things; but perhaps the wise minister – praying in an armchair and ready to sit in that chair and listen, encourage and guide – will be every bit as important.

Ministry in a complex world

It is neither honest nor creative to acknowledge the place of messiness and complexity in contemporary ministry and mission without facing certain significant ethical issues with which both the Church and wider society are grappling. While, as we have seen in Chapter 6, sex and sexuality have been dropped from the Alpha companion book *Searching Issues*, they most certainly have not dropped off the agenda of the Church or of society. A disciple-making church will need to engage in a hands-on and deeply personalized way with issues such as cohabitation, the place of LGBT people within the Church, assisted suicide, attitudes to immigration and women's ministry, to name just a few likely areas for attention. The list will vary from one church to another. Some issues – for example, immigration, relations with people of other faiths – might be high on the agenda of new disciples, but seldom seen as a source of anxiety by those well established in the Church. Others – including an extensive range of issues related to sex and sexuality – will probably not be seen as issues at all until new disciples encounter the disconnection between the Church's teaching and 'normal' life.

Discipleship may certainly involve individuals being challenged about matters of personal conduct, but if mission is a serious priority they will do so as belongers and not as outsiders. Any discussion, book or training package that starts with the question of how 'we' (the church members) relate to 'it' (the issues) or 'them' (people with the issue) will be heading for disaster. A disciple-making church will have living, breathing, praying Christians within it for whom these are all immediate and personal questions. If the doors of the local church are open, the messiness of life will be part of internal reality, not of the world out there.

The New Testament has valuable resources in an area that is not – currently at least – seen as controversial. 'Let the thief no longer steal,' wrote St Paul to the church in Ephesus.[18] Quite possibly a habitual thief was part of the fellowship, and a letter seeking the apostle's advice had made its way by foot or donkeyback to Paul, who had replied when there was time to write, and several weeks later the guidance arrived back in Ephesus, framed in far gentler language than Paul used when responding to sexual morality, disunity and gluttony in Corinth. There's no confusion – thieving is wrong – but clearly both local church and apostle were ready to give it time until the matter could be addressed. Meanwhile, living with a thief in the congregation seems to have been managed, although we have no access to the details of how that worked out in practice![19]

If matters of morality and behaviour need to be challenged in a direct and personal way in a disciple-making church, the challenge is not only one-way. New disciples will have their own questions to bring. The regular teaching of Jesus about wealth, of being unable to serve both God and money or of rich camels being unable to pass through needles' eyes may lead new disciples to ask some sharp questions to affluent congregations.

Serious shared ministry will inevitably involve letting go of power as new disciples bring with them new opinions, attitudes and insights. In some ways they will need to learn how the wisdom and practice of the Church, shaped through the generations, has much to offer. In others, the fresh eyes of new followers will spot the inconsistent, the irrelevant and the ridiculous. There is also a place for repentance, but if churches assume that this is the sole responsibility of new disciples, they may need to remind themselves that Anglicans have, for centuries, 'erred and strayed like lost sheep', and continue to do so.

The biggest challenge brought by new disciples is likely to be to the high cost and buildings-focused nature of much traditional church life. The usual assumption in village churches with church-yards is that if you love Jesus you will take on responsibilities, for example looking after the graves of those who have died in the parish through the centuries. It may not be stated, but it will show up in the church accounts. Those who come to faith and start the discipleship journey in an ancient church building may understand its significance. Those who encounter the love of God in Jesus Christ in the context of informal worship in a hired hall or a front room may be far less willing to see the value of ancient buildings, organ funds, expensive diocesan structures or synodical government. Each of these may be of great value, but a church of disciples will need to understand each of them, and either make a case for them or maybe have the humility to think how to leave them behind.

Leadership revisited

Ministry as shared discipleship may not easily fit within the paradigm of 'leadership'. The ministry of the ordained, along with a whole range of other recognized and informal expressions of ministry, may or may not be best defined as leadership. At any given time any player within the matrix of shared ministry may or may not be clearly seen as leading. Leadership may best be defined, in such a setting, as enabling movement in God's direction. Within that community, moving in response to God's leading, the ordained minister may be entrepreneur, releaser, connector with tradition, theological resourcer, question-raiser, or the person taking stock and preparing to help find Plan B.

As a recent report on the nature of leadership in the Church has put it:

it is a telling fact that the New Testament authors seem consciously to have avoided the most obvious words for 'leader' in their culture, presumably because they wanted to avoid buying in to the kinds of behaviour and organization that were associated with that language.[20]

If leadership is being exercised at all, it is with and within the whole Christian community, not above, not prodding from behind and not necessarily in front.

Francis Bridger, setting the context for the conduct of ordained ministers, has helpfully pointed to the work of Rollo May. According to May, power can be discerned in five categories:

- *exploitative power*, which dominates by force and coercion;
- *manipulative power*, which controls by more subtle and covert psychological means;
- *competitive power*, which is ambiguous since it can be used constructively where parties are relatively equal but is destructive where they are unequal (as in most pastoral relationships);
- *nutritive power*, which sustains and empowers;
- *integrative power*, which takes the freedom of others seriously and seeks to harness the other person's (potential) strengths.[21]

Historically, ordained ministers may have depended heavily on exploitative power, and skills-based training may enable short-term success to devolve from manipulative and competitive power. The power exercised by recognized ministers within the Church must find its home in the latter two categories, and will be destined for failure if it fails to do so. Disciples together will walk alongside one another as they follow Jesus. Exploitation, manipulation and competition are not the characteristics of that relationship. The nature of the journey will be far less predictable, but the chance of staying close to Jesus is higher if the way we walk, together, is closest to the way he walks. The future cannot be seen, but we can look towards it with confidence if we stay alongside Jesus, and it is towards that future that we look in our final chapter.

13

Back to the future?

——•◦•——

If I find in myself a desire which no experience in this
world can satisfy, the most probable explanation is
that I was made for another world.

(C. S. Lewis)

As we bring this book to a close we come back to the key question:
'How can we bring about the renewal of the Church, the growth
of the kingdom and a steady stream of new disciples for Jesus
Christ?' Simply to pose the question in these terms reminds us
that conversion and growth are not human constructs, but can
only come about as the gift of a loving and gracious God. But
that raises the question: 'Does God want his Church to grow, and
if so, why isn't it?' After all, God is all-powerful, and what God
wills God achieves, unlike the false gods of this world.

   We know from Scripture that God 'desires everyone to be saved
and to come to the knowledge of the truth' (1 Timothy 2.4), but
we also know from Jesus that 'the gate is narrow and the road is
hard that leads to life, and there are few who find it' (Matthew
7.14). God has given humans the gift of free will, which means
that he must sometimes watch sadly as people reject the offer of
life and walk away, as did the rich young ruler. But although God
wants everyone to be saved, that doesn't necessarily mean that he
wants everyone to join one of the institutional churches to which
we belong today. As Archbishop Michael Ramsey famously commented, 'I believe passionately in the One Holy, Catholic and
Apostolic Church and very much regret that it does not exist.' If
all our prayers for evangelism were answered, that might result in
a steady stream of new disciples, but they may not see the relevance
of – or be willing to pay to maintain – the heavily structured and

high-cost models of church that have nurtured and nourished our generation in the faith of Christ.

So if current forms of church are, as the writer to the Hebrews might put it, mere shadows of the heavenly reality that is to come, how can we help the churches of today to change in order to become more fruitful in terms of making new disciples, in partnership with the Holy Spirit, who is the agent of mission?

Towards the Conversion of England

In 1943, at the height of the Second World War, the Archbishops of Canterbury and York appointed a commission 'to survey the whole problem of modern evangelism with special reference to the spiritual needs and prevailing intellectual outlook of the non-worshipping members of the community, and to report on the organization and methods by which such needs can most effectively be met'. The commission's report, *Towards the Conversion of England*, was published in 1945 and dedicated to the memory of William Temple, who had died before its completion. Canon Max Warren, a leading overseas missionary statesman, described the report as 'one of the most remarkable statements ever authorized for publication by the Church of England'.[1]

In his opening address to the commission, Temple laid out two key principles for its work, the first of which was that the message of the Church is the eternal gospel, which could never alter, although the setting in which it was given and the method of its presentation could and did. These words call to mind the preface to the Declaration of Assent, familiar to Anglican clergy, which affirms that 'the Church is called upon to proclaim afresh in each generation' the unchanging faith revealed in Scripture. These words in turn inspired the phrase 'fresh expressions of church' in the *Mission-Shaped Church* report of 2004. His second key principle was that the first need in evangelism is for a quickening of spiritual life within the Church: 'We cannot separate the evangelization of those without from the rekindling of devotion within.'[2]

The report was widely circulated on publication; it was controversial at the time, not least because of the bold presumption in its title that England needed converting to Christ. Its findings and recommendations still have a contemporary ring to them. The very first recommendation was on 'the apostolate of the laity': 'the duty of evangelism is laid upon the whole Church, not only upon the ordained ministry . . . clergy must be given time to fulfil their primary responsibility of training the laity for evangelism.'[3] Seventy years on, religion may have a more marginal place in society and the Church of England may now be just one denomination among many, but its General Synod is still debating how to give the discipleship and ministry of the laity their rightful place in the life of the Church!

The report also urges the development of Christian cell groups in homes and factories, the continuation of Christian teaching in small groups after confirmation, the importance of ecumenical partnership in evangelism, the ability to engage with the new media (at the time it was advertising and the BBC), the need for a new catechism, flexible forms of worship for gathering in non-worshippers, simple prayer cards to help families reintroduce grace before meals and prayers in the home, a project on baptism to help families find suitable sponsors, and the appointment of a diocesan missioner in every diocese.

One significant omission from the report, pointed out at the time by the Scottish missionary and ecumenist J. H. Oldham, was that it failed to tackle the key issue of an effective apologetic. Without a critique of the prevailing philosophy of the times, it is hard to make well-grounded new disciples. Fortunately for the work of evangelism, a gifted apologist was beginning to make effective use of the medium of radio: in 1943, the year in which the report was commissioned, C. S. Lewis was in the middle of a series of broadcast talks that would later be published as the worldwide bestseller *Mere Christianity*.

The need for an effective apologetic is a point as valid today as it was 70 years ago. The contemporary focus on belonging coming before believing (though empirically true), and on reaching those searching for spirituality, carries with it the danger that people can find their way into the life of the Church without ever really having grappled with the historical and intellectual evidence for the truth of the Christian faith. Perhaps the rise of the 'new atheism' in our own day is calling the Church back to the importance of apologetics in any strategy for evangelization.

From our research for this volume we are aware that apologetics is still not getting the attention or resources it needs. Bishop Steven Croft, chair of the Church of England's Ministry Division, has described apologetics as a 'massively under-resourced' part of theological education in this country.[4] With the notable exception of the Oxford Centre for Christian Apologetics,[5] founded by Alister McGrath and Ravi Zacharias, there are few places offering training in apologetics for the Church today.

However, *Towards the Conversion of England* also recognizes that adopting the right strategy or putting in more resources will not achieve any results without a move from God.

> We cannot predict that, at any given place or at any given time, a new evangelistic zeal or new evangelistic methods will produce a commensurate movement of people back to God. Instead, the history of Christianity presents us with the phenomena of moments of Divine moving when, apart (as it seems) from human planning, and beyond human expectation, a man or a movement suddenly emerges, and a revival ensues out of all proportion to the quality of the human agency involved.[6]

Although much discussed, most of the recommendations of this far-sighted and far-reaching report were never acted on at the time – so much effort was going into rebuilding after the ravages of war, and William Temple was replaced as archbishop by Geoffrey Fisher, whose rather different passion and overriding priority was the revision of canon law.

'A necessary idiocy'

Various of the ideas contained in *Towards the Conversion of England* were taken up in the Decade of Evangelism, an initiative jointly owned by the main Christian denominations, though the Roman Catholics – and some Anglicans – preferred the term Decade of

Do we adapt the Gospel to our times?
Or will we adapt our times to the Gospel?

Evangelization. The concept of a Decade of Evangelism had its critics: Rowan Williams, then Bishop of Monmouth, described it as 'a necessary idiocy' – necessary because much of Western Christianity had gone to sleep on the job, but an idiocy because evangelism is so much of the essence of the Church that a decade devoted to it is rather like declaring 'a decade of breathing'.

The Decade of Evangelism succeeded in getting evangelism back on the agenda for the Church of England, after two decades in which so much energy had been focused on liturgical reform and the quest for visible ecumenism. This was no mean feat given the many other weighty issues competing for attention in the 1990s, such as the losses of the Church Commissioners, the ordination of women priests and the preparations for *Common Worship*. The Decade also helped to rehabilitate the word 'evangelism' for those parts of the Church for whom it had too long been identified with 'evangelicalism'. It didn't succeed in reversing decline in attendance, but it has left a major legacy in the attention given to the rethinking of the means of evangelism, in a changing culture. This was summed up by Robert Warren in his list of 'enriching trends in evangelism':

- From event to process
- From speaking to listening
- From doctrine to spirituality
- From gathered to dispersed
- From declaration to celebration
- From the search for truth to the search for identity
- From organists to orchestras
- From telling to living
- From verbal to visual.[7]

It is significant perhaps that apologetics, or equipping people to give a reason for the faith that is within them, does not feature in this list of enriching trends. Indeed, one of the trends is '*from doctrine to spirituality*'. If this is where the Decade has led the churches, then it hasn't equipped the Church to help people who are still wrestling with hard questions and seeking after truth to follow in the footsteps of Jesus.

Do we have a compelling vision
of what God is calling the Church
to be? Reform and renewal   *The Episcopal Church*
st. James Poral

At the time of writing, the Church of England is again poised on the brink of a new initiative from the centre aimed at making new disciples and growing the Church. In its initial stages the focus has been on a major research project to find out what makes churches grow[8] (on which we have drawn in this book), on a task group to share ideas on intentional evangelism, on recruiting significantly more ordinands, on identifying and training senior leaders and on reform and renewal of the Church's finances and governance, to simplify administration and more clearly align resources and priorities. These are all necessary steps for the Church as institution to become more efficient and effective in its core tasks. However, we have not yet discerned a compelling vision of what kind of church God is calling the Church of England to become.

'A poor church for the poor'

In seeking renewal and reform, the Church of England is not alone. Pope Benedict called a holy synod of bishops in Rome on the theme of 'The New Evangelization'. The election of his successor, the Argentine Cardinal Bergoglio, who took the name of Francis, the founder of the Franciscan order of poor friars, has seen the emphasis on evangelism continue, but also heralded a major programme of reform and a change of style and emphasis. Addressing a Church rocked by the repercussions of clerical abuse and financial scandals, Pope Francis has said that he longs for the Roman Catholic Church to be both poor and for the poor: 'Oh, how I would like a poor Church, and for the poor.' Eschewing the papal limousine and papal apartments, he has sought to model a different style of leadership. Without changing the Church's doctrine, he has sought to reach out to those who have felt most judged by the Catholic Church, including gay people and single parents. When he received a letter complaining that a priest had refused to baptize the child of an unmarried mother, Pope Francis telephoned her and asked if he could baptize the child himself, in the Sistine Chapel.[9]

'A discipleship movement shaped for mission'

The Methodist Church in Britain is also looking to its roots for inspiration as it seeks to reshape itself for the missionary task. Martyn Atkins, its General Secretary, points out that Methodism is, at its core, a discipleship movement and a disciple-making movement.

> Yearning and actively seeking to become better disciples of Jesus Christ, and offering Him to others, lies at the heart of being Methodist Christians. It resulted in the Methodist movement coming into being and my own view is that the future of Methodism is closely connected to the degree to which it is committed today to being increasingly shaped as a contemporary discipleship/disciple-making movement.[10]

To this end, the Methodist Church is reviewing all its work around the new strapline, 'a discipleship movement shaped for mission'.

Methodism was a movement long before it was a church, and it was a movement formed of people who wanted to learn together 'how to flee from the wrath to come'. John Wesley described a Methodist society as a company of men and women 'having the form, and seeking the power, of Godliness; united in order to pray together, to receive the word of exhortation, and to watch over one another in love, that they may help each other to work out their salvation'. Almost from the start, Methodists were divided into smaller groups, called classes, with a leader who would meet the group at least once a week to inquire 'how their souls prosper; to advise, reprove, comfort or exhort'. Atkins believes that the future survival of Methodism depends on its ability to rediscover its roots, lose some of its accumulated baggage and become again 'a discipleship movement shaped for mission'. This is a significant and inspiring vision that has much to say to all parts of the Church.

Missional communities shaped by prayer

So is there anything in the roots of our own denomination, the Church of England, that might enable us to reimagine ourselves for the task of making new disciples and promoting the common good of our society?

As we noted in Chapter 5, the Church in England owes its origin to communities of praying monks. When Pope Gregory sent his mission to the Angles in 596, he didn't choose a team of secular priests, but a group of lay brothers from his own monastery of Clevum Scauri in Rome, under the direction of Augustine; they also took along some English youths who had been bought by Gregory in the slave market of Marseilles. They were a fairly motley crew, coming to a halt soon after they had set out from Rome 'paralysed by fear', as Bede records; after they had arrived in Kent and were winning many converts, Augustine had to send to Gregory for reinforcements because, he said, the calibre of his monks was such that many were not capable of being raised to the priesthood.[11]

While southern England was being evangelized by the Roman mission, northern England was being converted by monks from Celtic religious communities, led by towering figures like Aidan, sent by Columba from Iona to found the monastery on Lindisfarne, and Hilda who, having been baptized by Paulinus, Bishop of York, went on to found the great monastery of Whitby.

The evidence we have surveyed in this book suggests that the future growth of the Church of England may come through the emergence of (largely lay) missional communities shaped by prayer. As we have noted, many lay people are being drawn to new religious communities, both gathered and dispersed, often lay led. In a culture that is starved of real community, where we are becoming a society of strangers and where increasing numbers of those outside the Church see themselves as being on some kind of spiritual journey, perhaps we need to pray more than ever that God will raise up women and men of godly depth, who can gather around them missional communities shaped by prayer. These communities may look less and less like rows of people sitting in pews on a Sunday morning, and may not be picked up on the average Sunday attendance measure, but they will be every bit as much disciples of Jesus Christ, bound to one another in a different kind of belonging.

The God who goes before

On the edge of Canterbury, well off the beaten track of the tourist coaches, lies the little church of St Martin. It lays claim to be the oldest parish church in England, and its squat, solid walls tell a powerful story. When Augustine and his monks crossed the English Channel we know from Bede that they expected death, 'going to a barbarous, fierce and unbelieving nation whose language they did not even understand'. However, when they eventually met the pagan king of East Kent, Aethelberht, they discovered that his wife Bertha, the daughter of the Frankish king of Paris, was a Christian. The treaty that lay behind this union specified that she was free to exercise her own religion, and to this end she had brought with her an aged bishop, with whom she used to worship and pray in the little church of St Martin, which dated from Roman times.[12] Augustine and his monks were allowed to use this church, and set about extending it and making it their base – the Roman building forms the chancel of the current church, and the extension built by Augustine forms the nave.

Here in this quiet church, still in use today, one is reminded that the evangelization of England owes much to the quiet witness and prayer of a foreign, lay woman. Bertha's prayers were answered by God with the arrival of a community of lay people from abroad, who had been willing to let go of all that was familiar and embark on a life-or-death adventure of faith. In the re-evangelization of England, the normative model of leadership may no longer be an ordained, English, male, but a lay, minority ethnic, woman.

The conversion of England is no more daunting now than it was in 596, and the God we serve has not changed. As he went ahead of Augustine, and prepared the ground in ways Augustine could not have imagined, so we dare to trust that God has gone ahead of us also, and prepared the way for us, as we will discover if we will but pray and follow.

Jesus said, 'Follow me and I will make you fish for people.'

(Mark 1.17)

God our Creator and Redeemer,
help your Church to grow in holiness, unity, effectiveness
  and numbers.
Draw us closer to you and to those around us.
Give us enthusiasm in our faith,
and wisdom in sharing it with young and old.
Open our eyes to new opportunities,
our lips to sing and speak of you,
and our hearts to welcome the stranger.
Grow your kingdom in us and in the world,
through the intercession of our Lord Jesus Christ
and in the power of the Holy Spirit. Amen.

(+Mike Bourke)

Notes

1 The challenge of making new disciples

1 M. Booker and M. Ireland, *Evangelism: Which Way Now?* London: Church House Publishing, 2003, 2nd edn 2005.
2 <www.ons.gov.uk>.
3 <http://bsa-30.natcen.ac.uk/read-the-report/key-findings/identities. aspx>. The latest British Social Attitudes survey suggests a further fall to only 17 per cent Anglican in 2014.
4 <www.brin.ac.uk/news/2014/british-social-attitudes-2013>.
5 R. Dawkins, *The God Delusion*, London: Black Swan, 2006.
6 Tweeted 10 November 2014.
7 <www.archbishopofcanterbury.org/articles.php/5098/there-is-a-revolution-archbishop-justins-address-to-synod>.
8 Pope Francis, *Evangelii Gaudium*, Rome: Veritas Publications, 2013, p. 3.
9 'The Seven Disciplines of Evangelisation', a discussion paper by the Right Revd Steven Croft, June 2013, p. 1.
10 <www.mobilemarketingmagazine.com/7-10-people-uk-now-own-smartphone/#Lg5gUZebitQUuHLb.99>.
11 <www.alpha.org/journal/feature/88>.
12 <www.anglicancommunion.org/ministry/mission/fivemarks.cfm>.
13 G. Cray (ed.), *Mission-Shaped Church*, London: Church House Publishing, 2004.
14 <www.churcharmy.org.uk/Groups/244926/Church_Army/Church_Army/Our_work/Research/Research.aspx>.
15 Archbishops' Council, *Statistics for Mission*, 2013.
16 B. Jackson and A. Piggott, *Another Capital Idea: A Report for the Diocese of London*, 2010.
17 R. Gill, *Churchgoing and Christian Ethics*, Cambridge: Cambridge University Press, 1999.
18 Gill, *Churchgoing*, p. 64.
19 *The Guardian*, 27 November 2014.
20 J. B. Phillips, *Letters to Young Churches*, London: Macmillan, 1947, p. xii.

2 The priority: growing the Church or growing people?

1 See, for example, J. Verkuyl, *Contemporary Missiology*, Grand Rapids, MI: Eerdmans, 1978, chapter 6; G. Van Rheenan, *Missions*, Grand Rapids, MI: Zondervan, 1996, pp. 38–43; M. Thomas Thangaraj, *The Common Task*, Nashville, TN: Abingdon, 1999, p. 152.

2 Robert Warren, in correspondence with the author. See also R. Warren, *Developing Healthy Churches*, London: Church House Publishing, 2012, chapter 6, 'Reworking Pastoral Care'.

3 Matthew 28.18–20; Mark 1.15–16; Luke 24.46–49; John 20.21–23.

4 J. Putman, *Real-life Discipleship*, Colorado Springs, CO: NavPress, 2010, p. 44.

5 See, for example, R. Cotton, *Reimagining Discipleship*, London: SPCK, 2012.

6 Church of England, *Resourcing Mission for a 21st Century Church*, GS Misc 810, 2006, p. 3.

7 G. Cray (ed.), *Mission-Shaped Church*, London: Church House Publishing, 2004, p. 85.

8 The title of his inquiry into the motives of the missionary awakening in Great Britain, quoted in D. Bosch, *Transforming Mission: Paradigm Shifts in Theology of Mission*, Maryknoll, NY: Orbis, 1991, p. 296.

9 Besides those already cited see, for example, A. Morgan, *Following Jesus: The Plural of Disciple is Church*, Wells: ReSource, 2015; R. L. Walton, *Disciples Together: Discipleship, Formation and Small Groups*, London: SCM Press, 2014; S. Reed, *Creating Community: Ancient Ways for Modern Churches*, Abingdon: Bible Reading Fellowship, 2013; J. Valentine, *Follow Me: Becoming a Liberated Disciple*, Nottingham: Inter-Varsity Press, 2009; G. Barna, *Growing True Disciples*, Colorado Springs, CO: Waterbrook, 2001; Archbishops' Council, *Called to New Life: The World of Lay Discipleship*, London: Church House Publishing, 1999.

10 Barna, *Growing True Disciples*, p. 20.

11 A. Hirsch, *The Forgotten Ways Handbook: A Practical Guide for Developing Missional Churches*, Grand Rapids, MI: Brazos, 2009.

12 Barna, *Growing True Disciples*, p. 35.

13 Church Commissioners, *From Anecdote to Evidence: Findings from the Church Growth Research Programme 2011–2013*, 2014, see <www.churchgrowthresearch.org.uk>.

14 Church Commissioners, *From Anecdote to Evidence*, p. 23.

15 Pope Francis, *Evangelii Gaudium*, Rome: Veritas Publications, 2013, paras 24, 40, 120.

16 Walton, *Disciples Together*, pp. 41–61.

17 Research by George Lings, Church Army.

18 The findings of this research at Willow Creek were replicated in surveys of 200 other churches. The survey forms used can be downloaded, for a (significant) fee, from the Willow Creek website: <www.willowcreek.com/resources>.

19 See, for example, <www.christianitytoday.com/ct/2008/march/11.27.html> and <www.christianitytoday.com/parse/2008/january/reveal-revisited.html?start=3>.

20 Rico Tice, address to Evangelical Ministry Assembly 2013, accessed from <www.proctrust.org.uk/resources>.

21 D. Everts and D. Schaupp, *Pathway to Jesus: Crossing the Thresholds of Faith*, Nottingham: Inter-Varsity Press, 2009.

22 Maxie D. Dunnam, *Congregational Evangelism*, Nashville, TN: Discipleship Resources, 1992, p. 48, quoted in C. E. Payne and H. Beazley, *Reclaiming the Great Commission: A Practical Model for Transforming Denominations and Congregations*, New York: Jossey-Bass, 2001, p. 130.

23 J. Finney, *Finding Faith Today*, Swindon: Bible Society, 1992, figures 15 and 16.

24 Church Commissioners, *From Anecdote to Evidence*, p. 26.

3 Strategy or spontaneity?

1 B. Jackson, *What Makes Churches Grow?* London: Church House Publishing, 2015, p. 84.

2 M. Chew and M. Ireland, *Mission Action Planning: A Vision-centred Approach*, London: SPCK, 2009, p. 10.

3 Ireland and Chew, *Mission Action Planning*, p. 59.

4 <www.southwark.anglican.org/what/Mission_Action_Planning> (italics in original).

5 See <www.ncd-international.org> for more information and details of the extensive and growing range of NCD resources.

6 R. Warren, *Developing Healthy Churches*, London: Church House Publishing, 2012. Not to be confused with the website <www.healthy-churches.org.uk>, which is actually a helpful guide to NCD from the Diocese of Coventry!

7 <www.liverpool.anglican.org/GPF>.

8 Details at <www.leadingyourchurchintogrowth.org.uk>.

9 From <www.commons.m.wikimedia.org> (exploring concepts developed by the Gartner Corporation).

10 M. Booker and M. Ireland, *Evangelism: Which Way Now?* London: Church House Publishing, 2003, p. 31.
11 Some material is drawn from personal conversation, some from Catherine Ellerby in the Church Growth *Resourcing Mission Bulletin*.

4 Jesus requests the pleasure . . .

1 See verses 10, 12, 18, 20, 21, 23, 28, 29, 30, 42, 43.
2 Parallel passages based on B. H. Throckmorton (ed.), *Gospel Parallels: A Synopsis of the First Three Gospels*, 4th edn, Nashville, TN: Nelson, 1979.
3 T. Horsfall, *Working from a Place of Rest*, Abingdon: Bible Reading Fellowship, 2010, p. 10.
4 E. H. Peterson, *The Contemplative Pastor*, Grand Rapids, MI: Eerdmans, 1989.
5 Matthew 15.24, 28.
6 R. L. Walton, *Disciples Together: Discipleship, Formation and Small Groups*, London: SCM Press, 2014, p. 10.
7 T. Cotterell and N. Hudson, *Leading a Whole-life Disciplemaking Church*, Cambridge: Grove Books (L7), 2012, p. 11.
8 D. Everts and D. Schaupp, *Pathway to Jesus: Crossing the Thresholds of Faith*, Nottingham: Inter-Varsity Press, 2009, p. 54.

5 God's work or ours? Praying for new disciples and spiritual growth

1 <www.biblesociety.org.uk/press/uploads/final-copy-of-Pass-it-On-research-report_02070706.pdf>.
2 G. Cray and I. Mobsby (eds), *Fresh Expressions and the Kingdom of God*, Norwich: Canterbury Press, 2012, pp. 108f.
3 Quoted by Archbishop Justin Welby, lecture on evangelism, Lambeth Palace, 24 March 2015.
4 D. Runcorn, *The Road to Growth Less Travelled*, Cambridge: Grove Books (S104), 2008, p. 10.
5 Runcorn, *Road to Growth*, p. 13.
6 Interview in the *Church Times*, 11 February 2006, quoted in Runcorn, *Road to Growth*, p. 18.
7 E. H. Peterson, *The Contemplative Pastor*, Grand Rapids, MI: Eerdmans, 1989, p. 36.
8 For details of summer ventures and Falcon camps for young people organized by the Church Pastoral Aid Society visit <www.ventures.org.uk>.

9 I. Adams, *Cave Refectory Road*, Norwich: Canterbury Press, 2010.

10 Morning Bell webpage via <www.iand.adams.info>; Morning Bell Twitter: <www.twitter.com/morningbell2u>.

6 Alpha revisited

1 S. Brian, *The Alpha Course: An Analysis of its Claim to Offer an Educational Course on the Meaning of Life*, PhD thesis, University of Surrey, 2003; S. Hunt, *The Alpha Enterprise: Evangelism in a Post-Christian Era*, Aldershot: Ashgate, 2004.

2 Published as J. Heard, *Inside Alpha: Explorations in Evangelism*, Milton Keynes: Paternoster Press, 2009.

3 Heard, *Inside Alpha*, p. 197.

4 Heard, *Inside Alpha*, p. 232.

5 Heard, *Inside Alpha*, p. 234.

6 M. Atkins, *Discipleship and the People Called Methodists*, at <www.methodist.org.uk/static/deepeningdiscipleship/discipleshipandmethodistsmatkins.pdf>, pp. 11–12.

7 Heard, *Inside Alpha*, p. 179.

8 According to HTB, on average 1,500–2,000 guests currently attend Alpha at HTB annually, and the total membership of their 110 ongoing 'Connect' (home) groups is also 1,500–2,000. Total membership of HTB is around 10,000 (source: Mark Elsdon-Dew).

9 Heard, *Inside Alpha*, p. 200.

10 See *On the Way*, London: Church House Publishing, 1995, and *Common Worship: Initiation Services*, London: Church House Publishing, 1998, p. 197.

11 M. Booker and M. Ireland, *Evangelism: Which Way Now?* (London: Church House Publishing, 2nd edn 2005, p. 30.

12 Interview with Mark Ireland at Alpha headquarters, 24 March 2015.

13 Interview with Mark Ireland, 24 March 2015.

14 P. Ward, 'Alpha – the McDonaldization of Religion?', *Anvil* 15(4), 1998, pp. 279–86; M. Percy, '"Join-the-dots" Christianity', *Religion and Theology* 3, 1997, pp. 14–18.

15 Script downloaded from Alpha website, 7 April 2015. These words are in red, and there is a rubric above this quotation that says, 'Delete red text if not applicable to your context, or amend the wording to use this as an example.'

16 Telephone conversation, 27 May 2015.

8 Fresh expressions: the way to the future?

1 M. Moynagh, *Church for Every Context*, London: SCM Press, 2013, p. 151.
2 M. Booker and M. Ireland, *Evangelism: Which Way Now?* London: Church House Publishing, 2nd edn 2005, chapter 11.
3 G. Cray (ed.), *Mission-Shaped Church*, London: Church House Publishing, 2004.
4 See <www.freshexpressions.org.uk>.
5 See <www.freshexpressions.org.uk/about/whatis>.
6 Church Army Research Unit, *An Analysis of Fresh Expressions of Church and Church Plants begun in the period 1992–2012: Report on Strand 3b of the Church Growth Research Project*, Sheffield: Church Army, 2013.
7 Church Army Research Unit, *Fresh Expressions of Church*, p. 44.
8 Church Army Research Unit, *Fresh Expressions of Church*, p. 87.
9 *Fresh Expressions in the Life of the Church*, report of an Anglican–Methodist working party, London: Methodist Church and Church House Publishing, 2012.
10 *Fresh Expressions in the Life of the Church*, p. 169.
11 Church Army Research Unit, *Fresh Expressions of Church*, p. 26.
12 Church Army Research Unit, *Fresh Expressions of Church*, p. 87.
13 Church Army Research Unit, *Fresh Expressions of Church*, p. 29.
14 See <www.encountersontheedge.org.uk> for the Church Army Research Unit's excellent series of accounts of some very varied forms of fresh expressions in existence. More recent reports are being added at: <www.churcharmy.org.uk/Groups/244968/Church_Army/Church_Army/Our_work/Research/Snapshots/Snapshots.aspx>.

9 Messy Church: Messy enough? Church enough?

1 M. Booker and M. Ireland, *Evangelism: Which Way Now?* London: Church House Publishing, 2003, p. 106.
2 <www.messychurch.org.uk/story-so-far>.
3 <www.messychurch.org.uk/messy-churches>.
4 Lucy Moore, *Messy Church*, Abingdon: Bible Reading Fellowship, 2006.
5 See, for example, J. Heard, *Inside Alpha: Explorations in Evangelism*, Milton Keynes: Paternoster Press, 2009, p. 114.
6 See <www.godlyplay.org.uk> for extensive information and resources.
7 G. Fisher, M. Hatcher, C. Hughes and L. Leech, *Lichfield Diocese Messy Discipleship Review*, Diocese of Lichfield, 2013.

8 Fisher et al., *Lichfield Diocese Messy Discipleship Review*, p. 15.
9 B. Jackson, *What Makes Churches Grow?* London: Church House Publishing, 2015, p. 173.
10 <www.acpi.org.uk/Joomla/index.php?option=com_content&task=view&id=220&Itemid=65>.
11 Personal conversation, December 2014.
12 Personal conversation, December 2014.
13 R. Hare and L. Moore, *Messy Lyfe: Living Life with Jesus*, Swindon: Bible Society, 2014.
14 Mark 10.15.
15 Fisher et al., *Lichfield Diocese Messy Discipleship Review*, p. 26.
16 <www.messychurch.org.uk/resource/ideas-boys>.
17 There is no central resource relating to this but it has close links to the Forest Church network. <www.mysticchrist.co.uk/forest_church> is a good place to start.

10 Parish: mature or stale?

1 G. P. Taylor, *Shadowmancer*, London: Faber & Faber, 2003, title page.
2 See <www.ncd-international.org> for resources.
3 The *Healthy Churches Handbook* is now available as a free download at <www.chpublishing.co.uk/uploads/documents%5C0715140175.pdf>.
4 B. Jackson, *What Makes Churches Grow?* London: Church House Publishing, 2015, p. 214.
5 See, for example, B. Jackson and A. Piggott, *Another Capital Idea: A Report for the Diocese of London*, Diocese of London, 2010, p. 37.
6 B. Jackson, *Hope for the Church*, London: Church House Publishing, 2002, p. 64.
7 Market research for the Christenings Project. Details available via <www.churchsupporthub.org>.
8 A. Barrett, *Making the Most of Your Child's Baptism*, London: SPCK, 2011.
9 One helpful booklet I have offered, among others, is W. Bray, *The Path Not Chosen: Beginning the Journey of Loss and Bereavement*, Farnham: Crusade for World Revival, 2010.
10 <www.soulfood.me/get-involved>.
11 Details at <http://seasonofinvitation.co.uk>.
12 B. Jackson and G. Fisher, *Everybody Welcome: The Course Where Everybody Helps Grow their Church*, London: Church House Publishing, 2009. More details are available at <www.chpublishing.co.uk/features/everybody-welcome>.

11 Good news: the hidden growth of the common good

1 M. Brown (ed.), *Anglican Social Theology*, London: Church House Publishing, 2015, chapter 1.

2 W. Temple, *Christianity and Social Order*, Harmondsworth: Penguin, 1942.

3 See discussion by Jonathan Chaplin in Brown, *Anglican Social Theology*, pp. 118–27.

4 *Who is my Neighbour? A Letter from the House of Bishops to the People and Parishes of the Church of England for the General Election 2015*, London: Church House Publishing, 2015, para. 5.

5 Aristotle, *The Politics*, Harmondsworth: Penguin, 1962.

6 *Compendium of the Social Doctrine of the Church*, Pontifical Council for Justice and Peace, 2004, chapter 4, part II, #164.

7 *Compendium of the Social Doctrine of the Church*, #168.

8 Search conducted 1 May 2015.

9 Archbishops' Council, 'The Church and the Common Good Today', GS 1815, *Challenges for the New Quinquennium*, London: Church House Publishing, 2010.

10 Statistic quoted by Archbishop Justin Welby at the Love Your Neighbour conference in Coventry, 21 February 2015.

11 A. Morisy, *Journeying Out: A New Approach to Christian Mission*, London: Continuum, 2006.

12 Interview with a Vatican Insider, February 2012, quoted in M. E. Bunson, *Pope Francis*, Huntingdon, IN: Our Sunday Visitor, 2013, p. 173.

13 *Who is my Neighbour?* para. 48.

14 See, for example, the Anglican-Reformed agreed statement *God's Reign and our Unity*, the ARCIC agreed statement *Church as Communion*, and the Meissen, Porvoo and Reuilly statements with the continental Protestant churches.

15 *The Common Good – The Church and Politics Today*, GS 1956, London: Church House Publishing, 2013, p. 11.

16 R. Fung, *The Isaiah Vision*, Geneva: World Council of Churches, 1992.

17 Morisy, *Journeying Out*.

18 For further information visit <www.besom.com>.

19 <www.trusselltrust.org/stats>.

20 Extract from a report on the *Cambridge News* website, posted 24 November 2014.

21 <https://capuk.org>.

22 From a video clip on the CAP website: <https://capuk.org/about-us/whos-who>.

23 In Brown, *Anglican Social Theology*, p. 102.

12 Church-shaped disciples, or disciple-shaped Church?

1 General Council of the Assemblies of God, *Pentecostal Ministry and Ordination*, 2009.

2 *Common Worship: Initiation Services*, London: Church House Publishing, 1998, 'The Ordination of Priests, also called Presbyters'.

3 Church of England Press Office, 'Signs of Growth: Cathedrals, Fresh Expressions, and Parishes around the Country Provide Grounds for Growth of Church of England', 16 January 2014, <www.churchofengland.org/media-centre/news/2014/01/signs-of-growth.aspx>.

4 See, for example, M. Breen and B. Hopkins, *Clusters: Creative Mid-sized Missional Communities*, Sheffield: ACPI, 2008.

5 M. Breen, *Building a Discipling Culture*, London: Zondervan, 2011.

6 Philippians 4.9.

7 Philippians 3.12–14.

8 L. Woodhead, *Church Times*, 23 February 2015.

9 Faith and Order Commission of the Church of England, *Senior Church Leadership – A Resource for Reflection*, 2015, p. 62.

10 A good example is Michael Lloyd, *Café Theology*, London: Alpha, 2005.

11 J. Finney, *Finding Faith Today*, Swindon: Bible Society, 1992.

12 Archbishops' Council, *Criteria for Selection for Ordained Ministry in the Church of England*, 2014.

13 <www.churcharmy.org.uk/Publisher/File.aspx?ID=138464>.

14 I am grateful to Dave Male for the observation.

15 M. Moynagh, *Being Church, Doing Life*, London: Lion, 2014, p. 265.

16 Faith and Order Commission, *Senior Church Leadership*, p. 16.

17 <www.freshexpressions.org.uk/pioneerministry>.

18 Ephesians 4.28 (RSV).

19 If the letter is a circular, as some commentators suggest, then the matter becomes even more interesting. Perhaps there were thieves in most churches!

20 Faith and Order Commission, *Senior Church Leadership*, p. 14.

21 F. Bridger, *Theological Reflection on Guidelines for the Conduct of the Clergy*, GS 1970, London: Church House Publishing, draft edition, 2014, p. 28.

13 Back to the future?

1 Quoted in T. Beeson, *The Bishops*, London: SCM Press, 2002, p. 202.
2 Church of England Commission on Evangelism, *Towards the Conversion of England*, London: Church Assembly, 1945, p. xi.
3 *Towards the Conversion of England*, p. 150.
4 *Intentional Evangelism*, GS 1917, London: Church House Publishing, 2013, para. 68.
5 <www.theocca.org/occa>.
6 *Towards the Conversion of England*, p. 145.
7 R. Warren, *Signs of Life: How Goes the Decade of Evangelism?* London: Church House Publishing, 1996, pp. 64–77.
8 Church Commissioners, *From Anecdote to Evidence: Findings from the Church Growth Research Programme 2011–2013*, 2014. See also <www.churchgrowthresearch.org.uk>.
9 <www.catholic.org/news/hf/faith/story.php?id=53862>.
10 M. Atkins, *Discipleship and the People Called Methodists*, <www.methodist.org.uk/static/deepeningdiscipleship/discipleshipandmethodistsmatkins.pdf>.
11 E. Carpenter, *Cantuar: The Archbishops in their Office*, London: Cassell, 1971, p. 6.
12 Bede, *A History of the English Church and People*, London: Penguin, 1955, pp. 68–70.

Bibliography

Adams, I., *Cave Refectory Road*, Norwich: Canterbury Press, 2010.

Anglican–Methodist report, *Fresh Expressions in the Life of the Church*, London: Methodist Church and Church House Publishing, 2012.

Archbishop's Council, *Called to New Life: The World of Lay Discipleship*, London: Church House Publishing, 1999.

Aristotle, *The Politics*, Harmondsworth: Penguin, 1962.

Atkins, M., *Discipleship and the People Called Methodists*, London: Methodist Publishing, n.d.

Barna, G., *Growing True Disciples*, Colorado Springs, CO: Waterbrook, 2001.

Barrett, A., *Making the Most of Your Child's Baptism*, London: SPCK, 2011.

Bede, *A History of the English Church and People*, London: Penguin, 1955.

Beeson, T., *The Bishops*, London: SCM Press, 2002.

Bergoglio, J. M. (Pope Francis), *Evangelii Gaudium*, Rome: Veritas Publications, 2013.

Booker, M. and Ireland, M., *Evangelism: Which Way Now?* London: Church House Publishing, 2003, 2nd edn 2005.

Bosch, D., *Transforming Mission: Paradigm Shifts in Theology of Mission*, Maryknoll, NY: Orbis, 1991.

Breen, M., *Building a Discipling Culture*, London: Zondervan, 2011.

Breen, M. and Hopkins, B., *Clusters: Creative Mid-sized Missional Communities*, Sheffield: ACPI, 2008.

Brian, S., *The Alpha Course: An Analysis of its Claim to Offer an Educational Course on the Meaning of Life*, PhD thesis, University of Surrey, 2003.

Brown, M. (ed.), *Anglican Social Theology*, London: Church House Publishing, 2015.

Carpenter, E., *Cantuar: The Archbishops in their Office*, London: Cassell, 1971.

Chew, M. and Ireland, M., *Mission Action Planning: A Vision-centred Approach*, London: SPCK, 2009.

Church of England, *Common Worship: Initiation Services*, London: Church House Publishing, 1998.

Cotterell, T. and Hudson, N., *Leading a Whole-life Disciplemaking Church*, Cambridge: Grove Books (L7), 2012.

Cotton, R., *Reimagining Discipleship*, London: SPCK, 2012.

Cray, G. (ed.), *Mission-Shaped Church*, London: Church House Publishing, 2004.

Cray, G. and Mobsby, I. (eds), *Fresh Expressions and the Kingdom of God*, Norwich: Canterbury Press, 2012.

Dawkins, R., *The God Delusion*, London: Black Swan, 2006.

Everts, D. and Schaupp, D., *Pathway to Jesus: Crossing the Thresholds of Faith*, Nottingham: Inter-Varsity Press, 2009.

Finney, J., *Finding Faith Today*, Swindon: Bible Society, 1992.

Fisher, G., Hatcher, M., Hughes, C. and Leech, L., *Lichfield Diocese Messy Discipleship Review*, Diocese of Lichfield, 2013.

Fung, R., *The Isaiah Vision*, Geneva: World Council of Churches, 1992.

Gill, R., *Churchgoing and Christian Ethics*, Cambridge: Cambridge University Press, 1999.

Hare, R. and Moore, L., *Messy Lyfe: Living Life with Jesus*, Swindon: Bible Society, 2014.

Heard, J., *Inside Alpha: Explorations in Evangelism*, Milton Keynes: Paternoster Press, 2009.

Hirsch, A., *The Forgotten Ways Handbook: A Practical Guide for Developing Missional Churches*, Grand Rapids, MI: Brazos, 2009.

Horsfall, T., *Working from a Place of Rest*, Abingdon: Bible Reading Fellowship, 2010.

Hunt, S., *The Alpha Enterprise: Evangelism in a Post-Christian Era*, Aldershot: Ashgate, 2004.

Jackson, B., *Hope for the Church*, London: Church House Publishing, 2002.

Jackson, B., *What Makes Churches Grow?* London: Church House Publishing, 2015.

Jackson, B. and Fisher, G., *Everybody Welcome: The Course Where Everybody Helps Grow their Church*, London: Church House Publishing, 2009.

Jackson, B. and Piggott, A., *Another Capital Idea: A Report for the Diocese of London*, Diocese of London, 2010.

Lloyd, M., *Café Theology: Exploring Love, the Universe and Everything*, London: Alpha, 2005.

Moore, L., *Messy Church*, Abingdon: Bible Reading Fellowship, 2006.

Morgan, A., *Following Jesus: The Plural of Disciple is Church*, Wells: ReSource, 2015.

Morisy, A., *Journeying Out: A New Approach to Christian Mission*, London: Continuum, 2006.

Moynagh, M., *Church for Every Context*, London: SCM Press, 2013.

Moynagh, M., *Being Church, Doing Life*, London: Lion, 2014.

Payne, C. E. and Beazley, H., *Reclaiming the Great Commission: A Practical Model for Transforming Denominations and Congregations*, New York: Jossey-Bass, 2001.

Percy, M., '"Join-the-dots" Christianity', *Religion and Theology* 3, 1997.

Peterson, E. H., *The Contemplative Pastor*, Grand Rapids, MI: Eerdmans, 1989.

Putman, J., *Real-life Discipleship*, Colorado Springs, CO: NavPress, 2010.

Reed, S., *Creating Community: Ancient Ways for Modern Churches*, Abingdon: Bible Reading Fellowship, 2013.

Runcorn, D., *The Road to Growth Less Travelled*, Cambridge: Grove Books (S104), 2008.

Taylor, G. P., *Shadowmancer*, London: Faber & Faber, 2003.

Temple, W., *Christianity and Social Order*, Harmondsworth: Penguin, 1942.

Thangaraj, M. Thomas, *The Common Task*, Nashville, TN: Abingdon Press, 1999.

Throckmorton, B. H. (ed.), *Gospel Parallels: A Synopsis of the First Three Gospels*, 4th edn, Nashville, TN: Nelson, 1979.

Valentine, J., *Follow Me: Becoming a Liberated Disciple*, Nottingham: Inter-Varsity Press, 2009.

Van Rheenan, G., *Missions*, Grand Rapids, MI: Zondervan, 1996.

Verkuyl, J., *Contemporary Missiology*, Grand Rapids, MI: Eerdmans, 1978.

Walton, R. L., *Disciples Together: Discipleship, Formation and Small Groups*, London: SCM Press, 2014.

Ward, P., 'Alpha – the McDonaldization of Religion?', *Anvil* 15(4), 1998.

Warren, R., *Signs of Life: How goes the Decade of Evangelism?* London: Church House Publishing, 1996.

Warren, R., *Developing Healthy Churches*, London: Church House Publishing, 2012.